This b...

George Philip & Son, Ltd

WOODROW WILSON

and

American Liberalism

is one of the volumes
in the
TEACH YOURSELF HISTORY
LIBRARY

Edited by A. L. ROWSE

Teach Yourself History

VOLUMES READY OR IN PREPARATION

[Frontispiece

WOODROW WILSON

and

American Liberalism

by

E. M. HUGH-JONES

Fellow of Keble College, Oxford: sometime
Rockefeller Travelling Fellow

NEW YORK

THE MACMILLAN COMPANY

1948

901
R79W

24920

Jan '49

PRINTED IN GREAT BRITAIN

To the
Yale Faculty Committee
for Receiving Oxford and Cambridge University Children,
and to the families of
Denis O'Connor, James O'Neill and George Shuster,
who opened their hearts and homes
to my children
during the Second World War

A General Introduction to the Series

THIS series has been undertaken in the conviction that there can be no subject of study more important than history. Great as have been the conquests of natural science in our time —such that many think of ours as a scientific age *par excellence*—it is even more urgent and necessary that advances should be made in the social sciences, if we are to gain control of the forces of nature loosed upon us. The bed out of which all the social sciences spring is history; there they find, in greater or lesser degree, subject-matter and material, verification or contradiction.

There is no end to what we can learn from history, if only we would, for it is coterminous with life. Its special field is the life of man in society, and at every point we can learn vicariously from the experience of others before us in history.

To take one point only—the understanding of politics: how can we hope to understand the world of affairs around us if we do not know how it came to be what it is? How to understand Germany, or Soviet Russia, or the United States —or ourselves, without knowing something of their history?

There is no subject that is more useful, or indeed indispensable.

Some evidence of the growing awareness of this may be seen in the immense increase in the interest of the reading public in history, and the much larger place the subject has come to take in education in our time.

This series has been planned to meet the needs and demands of a very wide public and of education—they are indeed the same. I am convinced that the most congenial, as well as the most concrete and practical, approach to history is the biographical, through the lives of the great men whose actions have been so much part of history, and whose careers in turn have been so moulded and formed by events.

The key idea of this series, and what distinguishes it from any other that has appeared, is the intention by way of a biography of a great man to open up a significant historical theme; for example, Cromwell and the Puritan Revolution, or Lenin and the Russian Revolution.

My hope is, in the end, as the series fills out and completes itself, by a sufficient number of biographies to cover whole periods and subjects in that way. To give you the history of the United States, for example, or the British Empire or France, *via* a number of biographies of their leading historical figures.

That should be something new, as well as convenient and practical, in education.

I need hardly say that I am a strong believer in people with good academic standards writing once more for the general reading public, and of the public being given the best that the universities can provide. From this point of view this series is intended to bring the university into the homes of the people.

A. L. ROWSE.

ALL SOULS COLLEGE,
    OXFORD.

Contents

CONTENTS

To the Reader

THIS book is a study of the United States from 1865 to 1921, a period during which the country recovered from the Civil War and became a World Power. Woodrow Wilson was the first American President to try to supply a comprehensive answer to the doubts and fears concerning the political, social and economic evolution of the United States which for half a century had been troubling American Liberalism. Some knowledge of the events of the fifty years before 1913 is therefore necessary to an understanding of Wilson, while his Presidency is of historical significance, not solely, nor even mainly, because of his participation in the international history of 1914–20, but because it is itself the culmination of a definite epoch in American history.

I am indebted to Professor K. C. Wheare for suggestions designed to improve the relationship between this volume and his own in this series. I am also indebted to Mr. E. A. Radice and to the Oxford University Press for permission to incorporate material from our joint book *An American Experiment*. I must particularly record my gratitude to the Director and Staff of the American Library at the American Embassy in London, through whose courtesy I have been able to borrow American books that would otherwise have been unavailable.

E. M. HUGH-JONES.

PARROTTS,
  WOOTTON-BY-WOODSTOCK,
  OXON.
August 31st. 1946.

Thomas Woodrow Wilson, 1856—1924

ON February 2nd, 1906, a dinner was held at the Lotos Club of New York at which were present representatives of the most powerful industrial and financial interests of the United States. When the time came for speeches, Colonel George Harvey, a political journalist and the friend and confidant of the great men of Wall Street, proposed as future President of the United States Woodrow Wilson, at that time President of the University of Princeton, who was among the guests.

This was a fairly long shot. Wilson was not an active politician, and Theodore Roosevelt had still three years to complete of his second term. But Colonel Harvey believed that he had found what his friends were looking for—namely a figurehead for the Democratic Party, who, while advocating government by the people, would not be able to prevent business interests from running the country. In the previous year the Republican President had thus defined his attitude towards Big Business:

1

"The great development of industrialism means that there must be an increase in the supervision exercised by the Government over business enterprise."

His efforts to carry this into effect had not seriously hampered business enterprise, but the view expressed was a popular one, and at any moment his enthusiastic nature might lead him to more energetic measures.

The Democratic Party was still hypnotised by William Jennings Bryan, the "deacon-desperado" of 1896, whose policy of cheap money had a powerful appeal to the masses. If, therefore, the world was to be made safe for business, what was wanted was a steady Liberal who would pass a few popular laws, but whose tenure of power would be otherwise innocuous and allow time for the wind of popular demand for "reform" to blow itself out. It was the misfortune of those who promoted Wilson's entry into politics, as of those who earlier had raised him to the Presidency of Princeton, that they did not realise his determination to be, not a figurehead, but a leader. It was Wilson's misfortune that he tried to base his leadership upon a community of moral ideas which he always assumed to exist between himself and the people he led, but seldom questioned how far these ideas were in fact shared by his followers.

At this time Wilson was just under fifty, and

his career had so far been of academic rather than of political distinction. He was born on December 28th, 1856, at Staunton, Virginia, in the valley where Stonewall Jackson achieved fame six years later. He had two older sisters and, ten years later, a younger brother. His father was the Presbyterian minister, and baptised his son Thomas Woodrow, the latter name being that of the boy's maternal grandfather, who had migrated from Scotland to the United States in 1836 and himself been a minister and theologian of some eminence. His other grandfather had migrated in 1807, and on this side the Wilsons were of Irish descent. This mixture of Scotch and Irish blood was a source of considerable gratification to the future President, who was apt to refer to it as explaining his natural obstinacy and combativeness. That it also contributed to his character elements of emotionalism and weakness was not so immediately apparent. By Article II of the Constitution of the United States the President must be a Citizen by birth, and Wilson, with immigrant grandparents on both sides, stands out, with Andrew Jackson, as one of the only two Presidents whose families had not been established in America for several generations.

Shortly after his birth, his father was transferred to Augusta, Georgia, where the family remained through the Civil War until, in 1870, they moved to Columbia, South Carolina, where

Dr. Wilson had been appointed to a post in a theological seminary.

It is possible to exaggerate, but equally impossible to overlook, the influence of these years on young Wilson. Of the Civil War itself he obviously can have retained little direct impression. When Lee surrendered at Appomattox on April 9th, 1865, Wilson was barely nine years old, and Sherman's destructive march did not pass through Augusta and was a subject of later reflection rather than of immediate observation. Nevertheless, Dr. Wilson must have often echoed in his own phraseology Sherman's dictum that war "is all hell." But the process known in American history as "Reconstruction" bore most heavily on South Carolina, and at fourteen young Wilson was able to appreciate what was being done to the simple society of the old South, while escaping the bitterness of recollection which gave so rancorous an edge to the opinions of those who could remember what Southern life was like before the war. Wilson's standard of reference was the simple disciplined life of his own family and the discourse of his father, whose wisdom, culture and Christian character profoundly impressed themselves on him. By this criterion he judged the changes going on around him and found them increasingly incompatible with the Jeffersonian form of society to which, in his latter years, he urged his countrymen to return.

4

While the Wilsons were not in the utter poverty of many Southern families, they were by no means wealthy. After brief periods spent in local schools a small legacy received by his mother enabled Wilson in 1873 to go to Davidson College, North Carolina. The following year his family moved to that State. His stay at Davidson was interrupted by a breakdown in his health, and he spent 1874 at home resting and studying. In 1875 he went north to Princeton College, New Jersey. Here he took his Bachelor's Degree without marked academic honours, although he had already begun to make a reputation for himself as a debater and public speaker. He had also drafted a constitution for the "Liberal Debating Club," which he founded in 1878. This seems to have been the first of his studies in constitution-making, which were to have an ever-widening scope until his final attempt at a constitution for world peace. For, from his early teens, Wilson was determined that, in one way or another, he would become a person of political consequence. Both at Davidson and at Princeton his reading was designed to equip him for this end, and at Princeton in the class of 1879 he laid the foundation of some of those friendships on which his later career was built.

Wilson's capacity for inspiring friendship, for gathering round him men ready to support him and to press him forward, is a striking fact in his life and in some ways exceeded his capacity for giving it. His deep need for understanding friends and his gratitude to them is a recurrent theme in his letters, but he was too apt to assume that they fully shared his ideals and convictions, and if disillusioned on that score, his severance of friendship was both ruthless and complete, and it sometimes looked as if he had no heart. He found it hard to believe that people who did not agree with him were not morally deformed, and this attitude of mind is not unnatural in a moral crusader, such as he was destined to be. One of his favourite passages, which epitomised the spirit dominating his life and was often quoted by him, ran thus: "Public duty demands and requires that what is right should not only be made known, but made prevalent; that what is evil should not only be detected, but defeated." For Wilson, political judgments were, equally, moral judgments.

This identification of politics and morals was perhaps an inevitable result of the impression which Southern politics, especially in the Reconstruction period, must have made on a sensitive boy who heard them discussed in the theological seminary at Columbia, South Carolina. During those years government had broken down in the South and public morality had been discarded. Among thoughtful men the belief that public affairs must not be divorced from moral ideals was a natural reaction, and in Wilson this belief was strengthened during his years at Princeton. In this and in many other ways he resembled Gladstone, who was his political hero—"the greatest statesman that ever lived." His political guides were Burke, Adam Smith, Bagehot, John Bright, Sir Henry Maine, and his ideal society was one inspired by their principles. The significance of Wilson in American history is twofold—first, that as a preacher of American Liberalism he began the task of welding it into a coherent system; and secondly, that as President he had the opportunity to practise what he preached.

Wilson's first aim was to become an active politician, and so, on leaving Princeton, he studied law at the University of Virginia. In America, as elsewhere, law is the high road to a political career, and in 1882 he joined a Virginia class-mate who had already settled in Atlanta to practise. As a starting-point for youthful ambition this city seemed a promising choice, as it was recovering strongly from the exhaustion of the war. Unfortunately for the firm of Renick and Wilson, there was one lawyer to every 270 persons resident in Atlanta in that year. It is thus not surprising that the firm's business did not prosper, indeed hardly existed, in spite of the advantage of both partners being of Southern birth and of an eloquent speech by Wilson denouncing protective tariffs and preaching the doctrine of taxation for revenue

7

only before a perambulating tariff commission, to which his attention had been drawn by Walter H. Page, then a reporter for the *New York World*. So, in 1883, Wilson decided to alter his whole plan of life and become a teacher.

In a democracy, the aspirant to political power may choose one of two courses. He may either become a politician, basing his power on his appeal to the mass of the electorate, or he may hold aloof from active politics and seek to mould policy by the provision of expert analysis and advice. William Jennings Bryan, a dozen years later, emerged as the finest American example up to that time of the former type. Wilson's decision to take the other course was due not only to the failure of his legal practice, but also to his fastidious disgust at the shifts and chicaneries which he found to be inseparable from the practice of law or politics when viewed at first hand rather than through the medium of books. He later found that academic life also has its politics, and when, later still, he himself turned to mass evangelism, his final repudiation by his countrymen was as spectacular as his first successes.

No such forebodings were in his mind in 1883 when he began graduate study in politics and government at Johns Hopkins University, Baltimore, where he took his Ph.D. in 1886. Between 1885 and 1890 he taught history and political

8

economy, first at the Women's College of Bryn Mawr, then at Wesleyan University, Connecticut. In 1885 he had published *Congressional Government,* his doctoral thesis, in book form. In this he expressed the view, which he subsequently tried to carry into practice, that the President of the United States is the leader of the American people and the interpreter of their will, Congress being the machinery whereby that will is translated into legislation. A further stage in the development of his political thought came with the publication of Bryce's *American Commonwealth,* which he reviewed in the *Political Science Quarterly* in March 1889. Bryce's book, which set out, as it were, the faith of American democracy, showed Wilson how inadequate that democracy was in the matter of works. "There still remains," he wrote, "the work of explaining democracy *by* America in supplement of Mr. Bryce's admirable explanation of democracy *in* America."

In 1890 he was appointed Professor of Jurisprudence and Political Economy at Princeton, where he spent the next twenty years. Five years before, at the outset of his teaching career, he had married Ellen Louise Axson, of Savannah, Georgia, who was one of the chief architects of his subsequent success through the unremitting care with which she looked after his always precarious health and provided a serene environment in which the flame of his particular am-

bition would never be extinguished. In time his
family numbered three daughters, of whom one
married William G. McAdoo, Secretary of the
Treasury in Wilson's Cabinet, and one Francis
B. Sayre, also a Professor of Politics, who later
did valuable work for the State Department. In
August 1914 Ellen Axson Wilson died, and in
December 1915 Wilson married Mrs. Edith
Bolling Galt, of Washington, who survived him.

Princeton in 1890 was still the old-fashioned
College of New Jersey, a rich man's college with
a strong Presbyterian tradition. It was for his
sense of tradition that the conservative President—Dr. Patton—had chosen Wilson, unaware,
as was so often the case with men who chose
Wilson for their own ends, of his deadly moral
sincerity. During his own lifetime, however, Dr.
Patton was able to prevent dangerous innova-
tions.

As a Professor, Wilson enhanced his already
rising reputation as a scholar and teacher. His
long face, with tight lips, reflected the severity
of his intellectual processes and, allied with a
strong gift of repartee, made him a difficult person to laugh at, while his natural but irritating
dignity of manner was increased by an occasional preciosity of speech—"Tommy Wilson's
jag of dignity" an exasperated friend once called
it. "A noticeable man with large grey eyes" was
Ellen Axson's description, quoting Wordsworth,
their favourite poet. But a moral tenseness

which could otherwise have been unbearable was relaxed by a vein of humour—rather than wit—which could be relied upon to lighten his lectures and after-dinner speeches. He was a wonderful mimic and fond of company and good talk. His lectures were not only eloquent, but also presented dramatically the issues of politics in a way which stimulated his hearers, but did not, perhaps, unduly disturb them. For while Wilson was urgent that a crisis was approaching in American society, his remedy was no more than an adjustment in the machine of government and an infusion of government with moral purpose. He was very accessible to the students, who regularly voted him the most popular professor, not only on the strength of his lectures, but because they remembered his record as a football coach at Wesleyan and how he had come to the rescue of Princeton football in the dark days of 1890, when all that was left of the championship team of 1889 was two men and the captain, Edgar Allan Poe, great-nephew of the poet. Wilson himself did not play football, though he had been a passable baseball player; at forty-two he took up golf, which became his regular relaxation, varied by an occasional hornpipe in the secrecy of the White House, for he was adept in what was known as "soft shoe dancing." He was also fond of the theatre, but, like many of his generation, preferred vaudeville to drama.

11

He was in demand as a public lecturer, so that by the time of his appointment as President of Princetown in 1902—the first layman to be so appointed—his views were already being listened to and he was well on the way to exerting a definite, if indirect, influence on the political thought of the country through a variety of channels. As President of Princeton he would command an even wider attention, and within ten years, first the Governorship of his own State of New Jersey—in which he had never been active politically—and then the Presidency of the United States itself became as much public offices which were thrust upon him as the objects of his conscious ambition. If in this he saw the working of Divine Providence, this was no more than Gladstone would have done, indeed frequently did, in similar circumstances. Here, however, the resemblance ends; Gladstone did not have to endure the torment of seeing his ideals and policies callously rejected by his successor in office; Wilson had to live through the Presidency of Warren Gamaliel Harding.

Wilson's tenure of his three great offices, between 1902 and 1920, constitutes that part of his life which is the most important from the point of view of history. In each case there is a pattern curiously repeated; first a period of initial success, when his impetus for reform not only carries popular approval with it, but carries opposition before it, followed by a moment when Wilson gathers his inner forces for the next great move forward and his opponents recover their breath, strengthen their defences and even prepare a counter-attack. It is at this moment that defeat is imminent and at this moment that on two occasions a new path opens, a way of retreat that is nevertheless an advance, first from Princeton to the Governor's office at Trenton, then from Trenton to the White House, to take him from the scene of possible failure. Only on the third, when his objective was not the achievement of an ideal university nor even of an ideal State government, but nothing less than the achievement of an ideal world order, there was no way of escape but death, and this was denied him, for the stroke which cut him down in the midst of his last campaign was not mortal.

PART I

The United States, 1865—1913

PART I

The United States, 1865–1917

Chapter One

Politics from the Civil War to Theodore Roosevelt

THE Civil War—which the Americans prefer to call the War between the States—is the leading case in refutation of the oft-repeated dictum that wars never settle anything. This particular war settled at least three things of major consequence for the history of the United States: firstly, that the States were to stay United and democratic; secondly, that the social and economic pattern of the country should be that envisaged by Hamilton rather than by Jefferson; thirdly, that the Federal Government was to be in the hands of the Republican Party for substantially the next half-century. We must consider these more closely if we are to understand modern American history, and Wilson's place in it.

Like all wars, the Civil War was the outcome of various causes, whose relative importance changed with its progress. Their analysis has no place here. Lincoln, in his speech at Gettysburg, reduced the issues to one, the survival of "a new nation conceived in liberty and dedicated to the proposition that all men are created equal." The abolition of slavery thus only appears as an incidental objective, since the "peculiar institution" had no place in a nation so conceived and so dedicated.

It is perhaps doubtful whether Lincoln equally perceived that the right of individual States to secede was at least arguable in such a nation and particularly in one founded on a Declaration that "Governments are instituted among men deriving their just powers from the consent of the governed, that whenever any form of Government becomes destructive of these ends, it is the right of the People to alter or to abolish it, and to institute a new Government." As a matter of sheer practical politics he saw that if the nation was to survive, then the right of self-determination must be denied, if need be by force, to any part of the country once brought under the Constitution, no matter what the Declaration of Independence said. Later this right was also to be denied to the conquered territories of the American Empire and to complicate the discussions at Versailles in 1919.

But the South—and this is important— accepted the judgment of the war and dropped its legal claims to secede. Henceforth the term "United States" was to be more than a mere geographical expression. How much more, time would show, for although the political unity of the country was now an accepted fact, there was still room for argument about the distribution of power between the Federal Government and the several States, which within the broad concept of political unity remained Sovereign.

Moreover, social and economic harmony had yet to be achieved, for there still remained the broad distinctions dating from within fifty years of the Declaration of Independence between the North-East, with interests primarily industrial and financial, the South, dependent chiefly on cotton and tobacco, and the Middle West with its corn, hogs and cattle. To these in time were added the Rocky Mountain group of mining States, and the Far West and Pacific group, cultivating fruit, vegetables, and timber. No region henceforward would attempt to secede, but in view of their different interests and even social patterns the unity achieved was hardly that planned by the Founding Fathers "fourscore and seven years" before Lincoln's Gettysburg oration.

Not only did the victory of the North establish national unity by force and at some sacrifice of logic, but it also seemed to fulfil Lincoln's resolve that "government of the people, by the people, and for the people, shall not perish from the earth." Yet as time went on, many Americans came to think that such things as the political treatment of negroes in the South and the dominance of politics everywhere by the pressure of business interests, of "lobbies" and "machines," could not be so described.

Secondly, the Civil War decided that the social and economic pattern envisaged by Hamilton and developed in the North should be extended over the whole country, although the political pattern remained Jefferson's. Jefferson, as a countryman, had believed firmly in the inherent common sense of country stock, and therefore advocated a minimum of activity by the central government and a wide decentralisation of functions, with the proviso that the nation should remain one of individual enterprises on a moderate scale and primarily agricultural. Hamilton, a New Yorker, had no faith in the power of the ordinary man to govern, and advocated a strong centralised government backed by the industrial and financial interests.

It might have been expected that since the Republican party was the bulwark of business and finance, the Democratic party would represent agriculture. But the Democratic alliance between the South and West was broken by the Civil War, and thereafter the agricultural States had no permanent political allegiance. The Democratic party in the North and East, so far as it survived at all, was the slave of the urban political machines controlling well-drilled blocks of voters having no interests in common with the South but the desire to get the

Republicans out of office. In the South itself the growth of industry produced no corresponding growth of Republicanism, since it was inconceivable, after the Reconstruction period, that any white Southerner should vote Republican. The result was rather that the Democratic party also became subservient to the influence of business and financial interests. Had W. J. Bryan been able, in 1892-6, to unite the farmers and urban labourers, he might have created a truly national party of the poor against the rich, but the financial resources of the Republicans beat him, and thereafter, as far as policy went, there was little to choose between the two parties, which were nation-wide but not national. In fact, the only real issue was which should wield power and patronage, since the Democrats, while saying that they wished to lower the tariff, failed to do so when they had the chance. It takes a strong, or at least an opinionated, President, if he be a Democrat, to oppose the financial and business interests—Republican Presidents generally do not desire to do so.

This industrial and financial leadership was what Hamilton saw as the future for his country, but it was combined with Jefferson's political democracy and a weak central government. Thus—and this is America's peculiar tragedy—a compromise was reached such as both would have rejected; Jefferson's political superstructure on an economic foundation he despised, the in-

dustrial and financial leadership desired by
Hamilton under a political system he distrusted.
The passage of time did little to alleviate the
situation, for although the States maintained
their exclusive right to regulate the new forms
of economic life, effective regulation was
hindered by inter-State jealousy and the difficulty of getting common action when each State
or region feared that if it acted alone, its neigh-
bours would reap an economic advantage.

Traditionally, the Democratic party is the
representative of the Jeffersonian position, the
Republican that of Hamilton. But, in fact, it
has been the Democratic Presidents who have
steadily expanded the Federal power, while the
Republicans have supported the doctrine of
States Rights whenever to do so would minimise
the likelihood of Federal interference with business. Both Theodore Roosevelt and Wilson tried
to solve the problem of how to regulate the
activities of business and industry, while keep-
ing within the limits imposed by constitutional
theory and tradition on the one hand, and by
political and economic expediency on the other.
It is thus a fact of importance in American
history that in the course of time the views of
Hamilton, even in the political sphere, have
been increasingly effective, even to the extent
of being followed in practice by Presidents who
claimed to be Jeffersonian Democrats.

Another political feature of the post-Civil-

War period was the change in the balance of power within the Constitution itself, a change which was the more harmful in that it took place not openly, but unnoticed and hardly recognised. The distinctive feature of the American Constitution is the care with which it avoids giving full authority to any person or group. Many important powers are reserved to the States, while in the central government authority is divided between the Supreme Court, President and Congress. But the Civil War proved that the rights of the States could be limited in practice by the power of the central government. Moreover, in this government the Supreme Court was not an independent source of authority, for it could be packed or overruled. It might exercise a delaying veto on the powers of Congress, but generally, as Wilson pointed out in *Congressional Government*,

> "it may be truthfully said, that taking our political history 'by and large,' the constitutional interpretations of the Supreme Court have changed, slowly but more or less surely, with the altered relations of power between the national parties."

Or, as Mr. Dooley put it more succinctly,

> "th' supreem coort follows th'iliction returns."

Thus the real division of power lay between the President and Congress, and in the early days of strong Presidents from Virginia and Massachusetts the balance had swung to the side of the President. Between Jackson and Lincoln, however, the Presidents had been figureheads, and after the Civil War Congress established its power against all but the strongest Presidents, and even then would only yield when the latter were able to mobilise strong popular support. Yet with this increased power there was no increased sense of responsibility, but rather a decrease both in the ability and character of the members, so that it was all too susceptible to external pressure. Wilson did not fail to perceive this conflict between Congress and President. It forms one of the themes of *Congressional Government,* and on the quality of Congress he remarks, with the somewhat dry humour characteristic of the book, that "The Senate contains the most perfect product of our politics, whatever that product may be." In 1912 he said in an address:

"The place where the strongest will is present will be the seat of sovereignty. If the strongest will is present in Congress, then Congress will dominate the government; if the strongest guiding will is in the Presidency, the President will dominate the government."

Not the least interesting aspect of Wilson's own political career is his attempt to swing back the balance of power in favour of the President.

Finally, the Civil War also established for several generations the political dominance of the Republican party. It was fifty years before a Democratic President served for two consecutive terms, and a further decade passed before another was elected who, by accident of war, was elected for four terms.

The supremacy of the Democratic party from 1828 to the Civil War had been based on the political alliance of the South and West, and by 1850 it had solved the main national issues of religion and the franchise, established political safeguards against the growth of an aristocracy and democratised the State Constitutions. Having then no national issues on which to pin its activities, it became sectional and traditional, and when the South decided to maintain the institution of slavery at the expense of the alliance with the West, the party collapsed. The rupture of this alliance was a prime failure of Democratic statemanship, and Wilson's success was due to his resumption of it and continued so long as he could maintain it.

The accession to power in 1860 of the Republican party and the triumph of their views over those of the slave-owning States was an equally sectional victory. At first their strength was based on memories of the Civil War, since it was easy to stigmatise the Democratic party as the party of treachery to the Union. As this phase passed, and particularly after the Presidency of Grover Cleveland, their strength was based sheerly on their success in retaining office. This in turn drew to the party the support of growing industries, by which in turn further success was assured, and its hold over New England and the North offset that of the Democrats over the "solid South." Though the Democrats obtained majorities in Congress, they failed to elect Presidents, and thus the party remained in the wilderness. While there was little to choose between the parties in strength of numbers, the Republicans had better leadership and political gumption and, most important of all, more money and influence behind them.

The "Reconstruction" of the South appeared to offer the Republicans a chance to reinforce their political supremacy in a manner which would not be open to them if Congress were to follow the policy of Lincoln's Second Inaugural Address (March 5th, 1865) of bringing the Confederate States back as soon as possible into normal relations with the rest of the Union. The Thirteenth Amendment had emancipated the negro, and the Fourteenth and Fifteenth were designed to secure his political enfranchisement. The Republicans aimed at ensuring a Republican majority in Southern elections by making sure that the negroes got their vote, and then that they voted Republican. The four Reconstruction Acts passed in 1867 and 1868 therefore set up governments based on the votes of the negroes and "loyal" whites, and also provided that no Confederate State should be readmitted to the Union or to representation in Congress until it should have ratified the fourteenth Amendment and the Amendment itself should have become a part of the Federal Constitution.

By 1868 governments as demanded by the Act were set up in eight States based on Republican majorities of whites and negroes and organised either by "carpet-baggers," political agents from the North or by "scalawags," Southern supporters of the North, who nowadays would be called "quislings." They lasted from two to nine years and were notable for grotesque corruption. The Reconstruction legislature of South Carolina, for example, consisted of 155 members, including 98 negroes, of whom 76 were illiterate. It voted itself champagne, hams, Brussels carpets, gold watches and ornamental spittoons under the guidance of a "carpet-bag" Governor, who himself accumulated a handsome fortune. Even when well-intentioned legislation was passed—for example in the field of education— it was nullified by misappropriation of the money voted for the purpose.

The more intelligent negroes, however, saw that such proceedings were an obstacle to their own advancement, while the less intelligent were terrorised by secret societies, such as the Ku Klux Klan and the Knights of the White

Camellia. Thus the Republican power in the South was paralysed at the source. The Fifteenth Amendment was an attempt to hold the ground, but it was ineffective, and gradually the white Democrats resumed control. By March 1877 carpet-bag regimes survived only in South Carolina and Louisiana, and by the end of April President Hayes, in return for the South's acceptance of his rather dubious election, withdrew the Federal troops whose support was essential to those governments.

Thus the Republican plan broke down, but it had, nevertheless, a lasting effect on subsequent American history, which cannot be understood without some knowledge of these few years. In the first place, it solidified the South in the Democratic cause—from 1876 to 1920 no ex-Confederate State voted for any but Democratic candidates for the Presidency.

Secondly, it shifted the problem of the negro away from the old simple moral ground of the rights and wrongs of slavery on to more complicated legal and social issues.

The importance of the negro population in the United States springs from the fact that it amounts to just under 10 per cent. of the total, and constitutes the largest minority group in a country of minorities. But its peculiar significance arises from this, that although the negroes were among the earliest of these groups to reach the United States, they have been an exception to the general rule that the coming of later immigrants raises their predecessors in the economic or social scale. Before the Civil War there were many people in the South to whom the situation of the negro was a cause of grave concern, and not a few who sincerely desired to see slavery abolished. Even if the person of the negro was unfree (though emancipations were numerous and increasing), he enjoyed the advantage of a clear and recognised position in the country's economic and social structure. While the picture must not be unduly romanticised, at least the chill winds of economic distress were tempered for him by a feudal paternalism. But the social and economic implications of the Thirteenth Amendment were not seen, and its passage left the negro with an indeterminate status and a dubious future, confronting social, political and economic situations with which he was not qualified to cope, for the South, while accepting emancipation, did not accept the implied corollary of social, economic or political equality.

By the end of the century stalemate was reached between the South, whose policy was "to keep the negro in his place," and the North, which was indifferent so long as it could claim that its own treatment of the negro was no worse. Since neither attitude was really compatible with America's creed of democracy, the inevitable result was an acute psychological tension which is still unresolved, and has influenced the attitude of Americans to their own rule in the Philippines and to British rule in India.

Thirdly, during the decade spent in the Reconstruction struggle, the North got a start in developing the Continent. While the Northerners were thrusting the tentacles of their railroads across the western plains and developing their industries under the protection of a tariff erected in 1861, and not substantially reduced till Wilson's Presidency, the energies of the South were monopolised by the effort of self-preservation. Thus the South remained socially and economically backward, and, even after the growth of its industries, remained the poorest section of the country. Finally, the effect of this period on young Wilson has been noted, and this too was to bring forth its fruit in due season.

The political story (excluding foreign politics) of the rest of the century can be briefly told. Andrew Johnson was succeeded by General Ulysses S. Grant, whose two periods of office are chiefly memorable for a series of financial scandals the like of which America was not to experience until the Presidency of Warren G. Harding. Of these, the most barefaced was the attempt to corner gold by Jay Gould and Jim Fisk—who was said to count among his possessions several railroads and steamboats, an opera house, a bevy of ballet girls and at least one bench of judges—an attempt based on the belief that the Secretary of the Treasury at Washington would not sell and so break the corner. This belief proved well founded, and the Secretary did not sell until after the operations of Gould and Fisk had almost produced a financial disaster. The trail of corruption nearly implicated the President himself. Members of Congress were known to have a financial interest in the Crédit Mobilier, a construction company organised by the promoters of the Union Pacific railroad as a means of increasing their profits.

Municipal government was also corrupt, and the "Tweed Ring," which held power in New York City from 1868 to 1870, looted the City Treasury of sums unknown, but estimated at between 45 and 200 million dollars. Business, in fact, was taking care of politics as a means of securing freedom from interference, and so politics became a business, the two powers allying for their mutual benefit. "Machines" developed to ensure that the voters voted right at the polls. These were more elaborate and professional than English political party organisations and were not controlled, generally speaking, by the party politicians in Congress, but by "bosses," who made bossdom a career and indeed rather controlled the politicians, through their skill in "swinging" elections and their knowledge of what was or was not politically possible in their areas. Of these the most notorious was Tammany Hall in New York, whose career as a political power began as early as 1800.

But the evil of the machines can be exaggerated. They might use crude bribery or threats or subtle methods of ballot-stuffing in order to "deliver votes," but also they looked after their people and served as relief and employment agencies long before "social security" was thought of. Martin Lomasny, sometime Boss of the Ninth Ward of Boston, put the point thus to Lincoln Steffens: "I think there's got to be in every ward somebody that any bloke can come to—no matter what he's done—and get help. Help, you understand; none of your law and your justice, but help." There lay the real strength of the machines.

In 1876 Grant was succeeded by Rutherford B. Hayes, of Ohio. Ohio is regarded as a lucky State from which to draw a Republican President, and Hayes was the first of a series which includes Garfield, Harrison, McKinley, Taft and Harding. Hayes started an attack on the Civil Service "spoils" system, by which government posts, even down to charwomen, were filled by political appointment, and thus their holders were liable to lose their jobs if the party in power were to fall. Although a sufficient cadre of trained men was always left to provide experience, the feeling of insecurity inevitably tended to corruption. Moreover, the need to dispense patronage wasted the energies of the President, who was its fount, for there were almost 120,000 executive appointments, and there were always several candidates for every job, and jobs had to be distributed equitably among the faithful areas as a cement to party loyalty. Hayes, however, accomplished little beyond the removal of Chester A. Arthur from his post as Collector in the New York Customs House, a post nominally under the Treasury, but actually controlled by Senator Conkling, a Republican boss.

For the election of 1880 the Republicans chose James A. Garfield, who was expected to satisfy the reformers without antagonising the supporters of the existing system. He was reported to be weak and not "alarmingly honest," and as a further insurance no less a person than Chester A. Arthur was nominated as Vice-President. Four months after his election Garfield was shot by a disappointed seeker after "spoils." Arthur, who thus unexpectedly succeeded him, with equal unexpectedness, considering his earlier career and the circumstances of his succession, himself continued the attack on the spoils system. In 1883 the Pendleton Act set up the Civil Service Commission and required that 14,000 posts, or about 12 per cent. of the whole, should be filled by competitive examination. The number of such posts could be extended by Presidents at their discretion, and was so extended by Grover Cleveland, Theodore Roosevelt and Wilson, so that by 1915 only about 10 per cent. of posts were filled by political appointees. Even so, the pay and prestige as compared with those of business were not high enough to attract able men. Still, morale and efficiency were improved, and, except during the administration of Harding, the Civil Service has withstood the numerous temptations offered by increased administrative activity. In 1882, under pressure from Arthur, Congress appointed the commission to study tariff revision which was addressed by Wilson on its visit to Atlanta.

In 1884 the Democrats managed to elect Cleveland, but in 1888 he lost the election to Harrison, in part owing to the publication of an incautious letter in his support from the British Ambassador, Sir Lionel Sackville-West.

For the Presidential election of 1892 the rank-and-file Democrats demanded and obtained the renomination of Cleveland. The Republicans could hardly avoid renominating a President of their own choosing, although embarrassed by a trade depression, attributed to the McKinley Tariff of 1890, which had raised the general level of duties from 38 per cent. to nearly 50 per cent. The election of Cleveland was secured by the influence in six States of the Populist party, whose spectacular rise can be better understood in connection with the economic history of this period, to be discussed in the next chapter. Down in Texas, Governor Hogg secured a second term of office after an election campaign directed by a young planter, Colonel Edward M. House, who had studied the mechanics of State politics and techniques of politicians for ten years and now began a ten-year career as organiser of victory for liberal and progressive governors. The Democratic revival swept into the Tennessee legislature a young lawyer from Celina, named Cordell Hull, while the newly elected city council of Nashville called itself the New Deal.

Cleveland's second term is remarkable only for his foreign policy (see Chapter VI) and for his failure to solve the economic problems connected with the panic of 1893. In February 1894 the House of Representatives adopted the Wilson-Gorman Tariff Bill, which placed basic raw materials on the free list and lessened protective duties, while losses in revenue were offset by internal taxes on various luxuries and the imposition of an income tax, the latter being the return made by the Democrats for Populist support. These measures were substantially those of Sir Robert Peel fifty years earlier and of Woodrow Wilson twenty years later.

When, however, the Bill reached the Senate, the assiduous lobbying of its opponents caused it to be altered, not merely in detail, but even in principle, so that when it finally passed into law, the general scale of duties was only lowered to 40 per cent. Moreover, in 1895 the Supreme Court declared the income-tax provisions unconstitutional by five votes to four.

To add to the difficulties of the Democrats, Cleveland decided that the financial crisis demanded stern measures and "sound money." He thus split the party between those who supported free coinage of silver and those who pinned their financial faith to the gold standard. In the Presidential election of 1896 it was currency rather than the tariff which was the main issue, but in 1897 the tariff was revised according to the Republican pattern in the Dingley Act, which raised the general level to 57 per cent. Thus victory lay with the protectionists, and as the following years were years of prosperity, the tariff ceased for a decade to be a public issue.

Yet the election of 1896 was crucial in American political history. In it the economic discontent of the South and West came to a head and found an eloquent spokesman in the young Senator from Nebraska, W. J. Bryan, who secured nomination by the Democratic Convention after a speech which ranks in American political oratory second only to that of Lincoln at Gettysburg. The Republicans nominated McKinley, "the man without an angle or a tangle," who was supported by Marcus Alonzo

Hanna, an Ohio capitalist and the greatest of American political bosses.

Against the 4 million dollars collected by the Republicans and Hanna from banking and business interests, the silver-mine owners could only provide the Democrats with half a million, and Bryan was beaten. McKinley rewarded Hanna with a seat in the Senate (Wilson showed himself less accommodating to the political boss of New Jersey), and, fortunately for the Republicans, an increased gold output at the end of the century removed the fear of monetary scarcity, while the failure of crops abroad raised the price of American wheat. Thus rural discontent was allayed, while the Spanish-American War and the colonial expansion which is the main interest of McKinley's first term were an added distraction from domestic problems.

At the election of 1900 Bryan was again the Democratic candidate. The main issue now was not silver, but American "Imperialism," concerning which the Democratic platform affirmed that "no nation can long endure half republic and half empire"—an ingenious echo of Lincoln. Yet, given a successful war and restored prosperity, the re-election of McKinley was a certainty, and with him, as Vice-President, Theodore Roosevelt.

Roosevelt's appeal was chiefly that of his own picturesque career—as a rough-rider in Cuba, a rancher in the West and President of the New

York Board of Police Commissioners. For most of his political life he had been a "regular" politician, but as Governor of New York State he had recently shown a deplorable interest in reform, and Platt, the Republican boss, was only too glad to have him kicked upstairs into the Vice-Presidency, which is usually a political backwater. In September 1901, however, McKinley was shot by an anarchist, and the plans of the Republican leaders to end Roosevelt's political activities were thus frustrated.

It is with the Presidency of Theodore Roosevelt that the full significance of the election of 1896 becomes apparent. For in the intervening five years the discontent voiced at that election had gathered strength and the Populist had been succeeded by the Progressive movement. These movements consolidated the Liberal wing of each of the established political parties. In Roosevelt the Liberal wing of the Republicans unexpectedly found its leader, and twelve years later the Liberal wing of the Democrats found theirs in Wilson.

Chapter Two

Growing Pains

WHEN Wilson was born, the Union consisted of thirty-three States, of which only Louisiana, Arkansas, Missouri, Iowa, Texas and California lay west of the Mississippi. When he was inaugurated President in March 1913, it consisted of forty-eight States. We are apt to overlook the fact that the final conquest of the natural obstacles to settlement and the integration of the government over more than half the continental area of the U.S.A. took place within one lifetime. In such spacious achievement the citizens of the U.S. found sufficient problems to occupy their minds, and they were thus generally less inclined than men of other countries to interfere in matters outside their own continental boundaries, save when their emotions or interests were violently aroused.

The South confronted the new era desolate and starving, for in the words of the Southern poet Sidney Lanier, "pretty much the whole of life has been merely not dying." The immediate result of the Civil War had been the break-up of the great Southern plantations and their replacement by small farms, generally held on a "share-cropping" system, which was inefficient and left the tenant perpetually in debt. In the lower South the number of farms doubled between 1860 and 1880, but they were devoted to a single crop—cotton—cultivated with primitive methods and tools and subject to the boll-weevil and competition from Texas. By the end of the century the total value of Southern farms was less than it had been before the Civil War.

Although some cities, such as Atlanta, recovered rapidly, there was little industrial development before 1880, but by that time the Southern cotton-spinning industry, which had been negligible twenty years earlier, numbered a quarter of all the mills in the country, and ten years after that one-half of the industry was in the South. By 1888 North Carolina claimed to have the largest tobacco factory in the world, while the lumber industry grew in Georgia and the steel industry in Alabama. In this way the South adopted Northern capitalism, but lost its own aristocratic order and culture in the process. The feudal conditions which in the South even more than in the North marked the growth of industry, allied to the mounting debts of the share-croppers, destroyed the very idea of a rural yeomanry such as Jeffersonian democracy had dreamed of. The South itself was less self-sufficient economically than in 1860, and because of its poverty a less-valuable customer than the

North had anticipated when it insisted on the indivisibility of the Union. It was rather to the growing prosperity of the West that the industrial North and East now turned for a market.

This prosperity was built around the railways which provided the arteries of the new economic body. In 1865 there were only 35,000 miles of track; by 1900 there were some 200,000, their construction being aided by loans and grants of land from the Federal Government. Although the objects of their promoters may have been as Robert Louis Stevenson said, no more than "a fortune and a subsequent visit to Paris," they did perform an invaluable service in opening up the country west of the Mississippi.

This had been traversed by explorers and occasionally by substantial bodies of migrants, as the Mormons on their trek to Utah; the discovery of the Comstock Lode in Nevada in 1859 had revealed the mineral wealth of the Mountain States; but the area was not yet occupied nor settled. The railways encouraged settlers and immigrants, who either bought from the railways part of the land granted by the Federal Government or took up a 160-acre holding under the Homestead Act of 1862 and other similar Acts. In turn the railways were able to open the markets of the East, and eventually of Europe, to the wheat and cattle of the Middle West, dealing a blow not only to British agri-

culture, but also to that of their own eastern
seaboard, where much land went out of cultivation and even reverted to forest, a phenomenon
to be repeated in the depression years of the
1930's. The railways also absorbed the output of
the growing iron and steel industry. By 1890
the capital value of the country's railway system
was around 10 billion dollars, and as railways
and Republicanism went together, it is significant that this sum was perhaps twice the value
of the slaves, whose possession had been the
economic foundation of the political power of
the Democratic South. It is also significant that
by the end of the century eight groups of companies controlled over half of the total mileage.

The agriculture thus developed was at first
primitive and on a purely subsistence basis. The
farmer's dwelling was, more often than not,
built of sods of earth—"the little old sod-shanty
on my claim" of local folk-song—and living conditions were unbelievably hard on men and
women alike. But in the ensuing thirty years
the use of machinery grew and the amount of
capital invested in agriculture grew likewise,
and land values rose after 1890, when the Census
Bureau announced that "the unsettled area has
been so broken into by isolated bodies of settlement that there can hardly be said to be a
frontier line." The growing volume of agricultural produce provided freight for the railways
and food for factory workers, and in return the

factories supplied farm implements and, no less
important, barbed wire. American economic
independence was aided by the export of
wheat, which discharged her debts to Europe.
At the same time the agricultural areas tended
to become specialised. With the spread of the
railways, the centre of her wheat production
moved from Illinois and Iowa to the Dakotas.
Corn production centred in Kansas and
Nebraska, becoming meat via hogs and the packing plants of Chicago and Kansas City. Similarly
in the South corn and wheat production yielded
to cotton. With single-crop agriculture and
rising land values the farmer's self-sufficiency
steadily vanished, and his dependency on the
banks increased. The old Jeffersonian dream
of farms worked by independent owners and
their families was giving way to the reality of a
tenant-farmer with a mortgage, although the
final dissolution of this dream was not to come
till the lean years of the 1920's.

The most picturesque, if the shortest-lived,
aspect of American agriculture was the prairie
period of the cattle industry. Texas cattle had a
more distinguished lineage than even those of
their consumers who could trace descent from
the Pilgrim Fathers, for the ancestors of the
cattle had come over with Columbus. Hitherto,
however, they had been chiefly valued for their
hides. But in the nineteenth century crossing
with Herefords had produced the famous breed

43

of Texas Longhorn, and in 1866 it was discovered that beef cattle could be driven north across the unfenced public domain and arrive at railhead "cow towns" larger and fatter than when they started. From the railheads they could then be transported to the stockyards, where they were slaughtered and dressed and sent to eastern and subsequently to world markets in refrigerated cars or in cans. The demand for fresh beef from railroad labourers and mining camps and the improved marketing facilities provided by the completion of the railroads fostered the expansion of the industry, and, so long as the prairies were unfenced and pasturage was free, cattle were a good investment. A few cowboys could handle enormous herds raised on the open plains, which the cattlemen treated as their own, and the indigenous buffalo was crowded out or exterminated by the hunters, of whom the most famous was Buffalo Bill, a scout employed by the Kansas Pacific Railway, who slew 4,280 in eighteen months.

The big event of the year was the spring round-up, when calves were branded and the steers started along the various trails on the long drive from Texas to Wyoming. In a peak year nearly a million head of cattle would be moved north by several thousand cowboys, but after 1885 the range became intersected by the railways and by the barbed-wire fences of the advancing homesteaders. After a brief struggle the cattlemen had to abandon the open range and the long drive and set up fixed ranches, and as the cattle industry became static it lost its colour and romance.

But not all the colour was provided by the cowboys. The mining era also made its romantic contribution in the various "rushes" of intrepid prospectors for gold or silver, whose avowed aim, as in 1859, was "Pike's Peak or Bust." Most of the miners did indeed bust, but they opened up the Far West and showed the way for the more solid exploiters of the natural wealth of Montana, Colorado, Idaho and California. The rise of gold and silver mining enabled the paper currency of the Civil War period to be redeemed in bullion and brought the money question into American politics. Silver has never entirely lost its political significance, though economically it is not so important as the baser metals, or as oil or coal.

During 1890 to 1900 the Mesabi range, situated on the watershed of the Mississippi, Rainy and St. Louis rivers, provided 40 million tons of iron ore for conversion into steel, first by the Bessemer and later by the open-hearth process. Oil was found in Pennsylvania in 1859 and its production was well developed five years later, while inexhaustible supplies of coal were available in Pennsylvania, West Virginia, along the Great Smokies and in Kansas, Colorado,

Texas and New Mexico, together with vast resources of natural gas. By 1900 the United States was one of the world's great manufacturing countries and the process of industrial expansion had drawn half of the population into the cities. The average American was no longer a yeoman farmer, but an employee.

While the development of the continent was thus proceeding at an almost torrential pace, certain solid problems were emerging, like rocks in a rushing stream, to create the swirls and eddies of economic and political controversy. These were the problems of natural resources, of silver, tariffs and banking, and of "Trusts."

To the Americans of the closing decades of the nineteenth century the resources of the country appeared infinite and economy seemed unnecessary. The waste of resources was, therefore, colossal. Forests were devastated with no thought of replacement. The development of single-crop agriculture not merely made the economy of the various areas inflexible, but deprived the soil of the physical benefits of crop rotation and prepared the way for the erosion which was to become critical in the next century. The wanton destruction of the buffalo on the western plains was the preliminary to the conversion of those plains from long-rooted grasslands to shallow-rooted cornlands, and subsequently to the "Dust Bowls" of to-day. Wells were drilled for oil equally regardless of

46

their effect on the underlying oil-bed as of their effect on the economics of the industry, and the water-power of mighty rivers was not only un-utilised, but left to create periodic inundations. Nevertheless, it was not until the Presidency of Theodore Roosevelt that any attempt was made to formulate a conservation policy, and it is still incomplete.

With the problem of silver we return to the nineteenth century. For the first three-quarters of that century the United States was a bi-metallist country, the ratio of gold to silver being fixed at fifteen to one. The paper finance of the Civil War brought about a period of cheap money and high prices, but when it was over the government called in a good proportion of the "greenback" currency and followed a policy of deflation, to the advantage of creditors and investors, but to the disadvantage of farmers and labourers. Between the supporters of a con-tinuance of cheap money and those who wanted a more rigid policy a great struggle developed. By 1873 the increasing output of the American silver mines, combined with the abandonment of bi-metallism in favour of the gold standard by various European countries, had reduced the price of silver and destroyed the old ratio with gold. In that year Congress passed the Coinage Act, which made no provision for the coinage of silver dollars, and thus demonetised silver. By the silver-mining interests this was regarded as a "crime," and as deflation reduced agricultural prices, the farmers of the South and West joined them in demanding free and unlimited coinage of silver as a means of restoring the price-level.

In 1890 the silver interests forced through Congress the Sherman Silver Purchase Act, requiring the government to buy at the market rate $4\frac{1}{2}$ million ounces of silver a month, or practically the whole American output. Two years later the Populist Party adopted silver as the main plank in their platform, but in the crisis of 1893 President Cleveland had the Sherman Act repealed at the cost of splitting the Democratic party. The defeat of the Democrats in 1896 ended "free silver" as a practical political issue, but it had played its part in the development of American Liberalism because it dramatised the fact that there were in America, as in England, Two Nations—the financiers and industrialists of Hamilton, and the ordinary farmers and workmen of Jefferson. Only disbelief in the inevitability of poverty prevented Americans from identifying these with the Two Nations of Disraeli's *Sybil*.

Up to the Civil War banking was essentially a local matter, and all banks enjoyed and exercised the privilege of issuing currency notes. In 1863 a "National" system was set up—that is to say, local banking associations under Federal authority were empowered to issue notes backed by Federal securities, which the banks purchased. In 1865 Congress, by taxing the notes of the other banks, successfully stopped their issue. But we must not be confused by mere names. The "State" banks continued their business merely shorn of note-issuing powers. The so-called "National" banks were no less local, and both were privately owned. For each kind of bank the limit of its activity was the State boundary, and each bank functioned as a separate entity, branch banking beyond State boundaries being forbidden. There was no national central bank comparable to the Bank of England, and the control exercised by the Federal Government over banking operations was so tenuous as to be practically non-existent. This highly individualist system, if it can be called a system, remained unchanged until Wilson's Presidency. Its result was an inflexibility in the currency which both increased the violence of economic crises and made impossible any conscious attempt to control them.

We have already outlined the gradual rise in the level of the tariff during this period. Behind the tariff wall, though by no means uniquely because of it, developed those consolidations of industry and later of finance whose liquidation was the main objective of Liberal reformers. These consolidations, whatever there actual form, were generally known as "Trusts."

The movement began on the railroads and spread into almost every branch of American industry, "from meat to tombstones." The most famous and most hated was the Standard Oil Company, organised by John D. Rockefeller in 1870. By 1872 Rockefeller had acquired complete control of the Cleveland Oil refineries, and by the time the Standard Oil Trust was organised ten years later it had a practical monopoly of the refining and transport of oil. In 1890 the Ohio Supreme Court ordered its dissolution, but the Trust retained its character, and in 1899 reincorporated under the laws of New Jersey as a holding company. In 1907 it was fined $29,240,000, and in 1911 its dissolution was again ordered, this time by the Supreme Court of the United States. Nevertheless, in 1913 it declared a 60 per cent. dividend and in 1922 a 400 per cent. stock dividend.

If the Standard Oil Trust owed little to the tariff, the Steel Trust owed much. Protected from foreign competition by prohibitive import duties, Andrew Carnegie was able to establish a vertical combination controlling all the materials and stages of steel-making—the ore, coal and coke, transport to take them to the foundries, the foundries themselves, the mills and the finished article. Labour was recruited at cheap rates from the successive waves of immigrants, frequently housed in company-dominated towns, and worked for twelve hours a day seven days a week (this continued till 1923, although in the majority of industries the

ten-hour day had been established by 1890 and
by 1920 nearly half of all factory wage-earners
were on an eight-hour day or 44–48-hour week).
In 1901 the United States Steel Corporation was
formed with a capital of $1,400 million dollars,
or more than the total national wealth a century
earlier; it absorbed or eliminated most of the
six hundred individual iron and steel firms who
had at one time shared the field with Carnegie.

Other Trusts were the Sugar, Tobacco, Beef,
Salt and Whisky Trusts, the Western Union
Telegraph Company, the American Telegraph
and Telephone Company and the railroad combinations already mentioned. By the turn of the
century some three hundred industrial Trusts
with an average capital value of 20 million
dollars apiece had swallowed up over five thousand previously independent concerns.

Money was the cement of these colossal
amalgamations, and it was only natural that the
control of money should also come to centre in
a few hands. In 1864 J. Pierpont Morgan had
been placed in charge of the American branch
of the Morgan interests then based on London.
Nine years later he was responsible for re-
financing 375 million dollars of the American
national debt, and the bankruptcy the same year
of Jay Cooke, his only rival, left him supreme
in the field. The House of Morgan, domiciled
at Number 23 Wall Street, in a five-storey building "impersonal to an almost forbidding

degree" among the pretentious and surrounding
sky-scrapers, arranged the incorporation of U.S.
Steel, International Harvester and many other
of the big combines not unprofitably to itself.
Woodrow Wilson might state that "the great
monopoly in this country is the money monopoly" and the Pujo Committee of 1911 reveal
that the Morgan and William Rockefeller interests between them held 341 directorships in
a variety of companies with total resources
amounting to 22,000 million dollars, but the
House of Morgan survived that Committee and
another one twenty years later.

The growth of these giant concerns presented
the American people with an awkward problem.
On the one hand, they undoubtedly promoted
efficiency by the elimination of those unfit to
survive and provided the mass output necessary
to meet the needs of a rapidly expanding population. Their vast resources made possible industrial and scientific research on an extensive
scale which in turn should lead to more and
even better products. Moreover, and paradoxically, they appeared to vindicate the American
dream of freedom and the illimitable opportunities open to the individual who cared to take
them, for had not Carnegie entered the country
as a penniless lad of twelve and the great
Cornelius Vanderbilt of the New York Central
Railroad system started on his way to wealth by
ferrying passengers across New York harbour in

a small rowing-boat? On the other hand, they drove hard bargains with labour and the public; local industry withered under their shadow or was forced under the absentee control of distant financiers. Their desire to be free from outside interference led them to permeate and corrupt State and even National politics and control legislatures and the judiciary. "Law," said Cornelius Vanderbilt. "What do I care about law? Hain't I got the power?" A State within the State was seen to be growing up and it was not made a democratic one by the fact that shares in the corporations were often widely held; on the contrary, just because the shareholders were numbered by the hundred thousand, centralised control by a minority was actually easier. Power was being concentrated in a few key points and the many were being controlled by the few more effectively than ever before. It was this thought that the Liberal reformers found so disturbing, for if it were true, then the "American Dream" of individual freedom and equal opportunity was not, in fact, being realised.

Chapter Three

The Age of Protest

THE story of American Liberalism is the story of a succession of protests against one or other of those aspects of American development noted in the last chapter—protests which begin with the half-comprehending agitation of the farmers, become coherent and vocal with the Populist movement and the growth of organised labour, and rise to a thunderous roar in the great election of 1896. Then, after an interval, there is the steady drive of the Progressive movement through the Presidencies of Theodore Roosevelt, Taft and Wilson until the youthful enthusiasm becomes pale and spectre-thin and dies in the Republican era of the nineteen-twenties.

The problem of the American farmer was how to make a living when he alone could not fix the price of what he had to sell, but had to take what his crops would fetch when they reached the market, while if he wanted farm implements, barbed wire or fertiliser, he had to pay the price fixed by the trusts, and when he came to send his crops to market, the freight charges were fixed at a monopoly level by the

54

railroads. If he wanted to borrow money, the inadequacies of the banking system forced him to pay high rates of interest, and whenever prices fell, his debts increased. Prices, indeed, seemed to be always falling, especially in the early seventies and again in the late eighties, and on each occasion the result was to intensify agitation in the farming States.

Thus the fall of prices after the panic of 1873 stimulated the political and economic activities of the "Grange" movement which had started some seven years earlier for social purposes and to provide co-operative buying organisations and factories to supply their members' needs. These latter mostly failed in a few years, but they did something to bring down manufacturers' prices and were also responsible for the starting of the great mail-order houses, whose ever-widening range of goods did much to transform and ameliorate the conditions of American agricultural life, as their ever-expanding catalogues became, with the Bible, the staple reading of the farming belt. The Granges also began to exert political influence, and in some Mid-Western States regulated oppressive railroad and warehouse charges either directly by "Granger Laws" or indirectly by the establishment of Commissions. But as prosperity returned, the activities of the Granges died down or merged with those of the "Greenback" party and the agitation for free silver.

The Greenback party was organised in 1875 to demand the reissue of paper money as a means of inflating the currency and of raising prices. Five years later it chose as Presidential candidate an old "Granger," J. B. Weaver, of Iowa, who had little success in that election but as a Populist candidate did secure twenty-two electoral votes in the election of 1892. The Greenback movement itself was soon swamped in the silver movement the cause of whose rise has already been briefly sketched. Besides the reasons then given, we may here note that in the eighties the surplus revenue of the Federal Government enabled it to retire a quantity of its bonds, and as these were the basis of the National Bank notes, the volume of the latter was reduced.

This was one cause of the fall in prices, which was accentuated for the farmers by droughts in Kansas and Nebraska from 1883 to 1889, whereby corn yields were reduced and the farmers driven deeper into debt and mortgages. This, in its turn, led to a reappearance of farmers' organisations, and by 1888 the "Southern Farmers' Alliance" covered the Southern cotton belt and the "Northern Farmer's Alliance" the Middle West. Advised by Mrs. Mary E. Leese to "raise less corn and more hell," they turned away from co-operative commercial ventures and became increasingly political. The legislative result of this unrest was the Interstate Commerce Act of 1887 and the Sherman Anti-Trust Act of 1890, while the passage of the Sherman Silver Purchase Act in 1890 was due to their co-operation with the Silver party, whose strength in Congress had just been increased by the representatives of the six Western States admitted to the Union in 1889–1890. Farmers also provided the voting weight behind the Populist party, whose programme in the Presidential campaign of 1892 voiced their complaints and remedies, and indeed the general apprehension that though negro slavery had been abolished, a new slavery of the whole nation had taken its place, a slavery resulting from the aggregation of capital and the control of business into the hands of a few men.

For at least a dozen years Bills for the national regulation of railways had been passed either by the House of Representatives or by the Senate, but since they were never the same Bills, they never became Acts. However, in 1887 Congress passed the Interstate Commerce Act, which provided that rates and charges "shall be reasonable and just" and should be published, and set up the Interstate Commerce Commission to investigate complaints and to bring actions in the Federal Courts. Although the Act was not particularly successful, yet the principle of national regulation was established and machinery set up for use when wanted.

As with the railways, so with business,

attempts had been made by State and Municipal enactments to satisfy the public demand for regulation. But trusts and combinations attacked in one State could always resume their outlawed practices by dissolving and reincorporating under the laws of some more complaisant State, since charters granted in any State were universally valid. Thus although in 1886–90 there was a general movement of State legislation to prevent agreements in restraint of trade, the fact that New Jersey, Delaware and West Virginia stayed out made these local measures relatively ineffectual.

It was in an attempt to improve the situation that Congress passed the Sherman Anti-Trust Act of 1890, which enacted that

> "Every contract, combination in the form of a trust or otherwise, or conspiracy in restraint of trade or commerce among the several states, or with foreign nations, is hereby declared to be illegal."

But in 1895 the Supreme Court, in the case of the U.S. v. E. C. Knight Co. held that, although the Sugar Trust controlled 98 per cent. of the sugar refining of the country, this did not violate the Sherman Act. This decision virtually killed the Act for the time being, and the ensuing decade witnessed the creation of more combinations than ever before. But if the Act was powerless to restrain business, it was powerful against labour, and until the Presidency of Theodore Roosevelt was more vigorously used against trade unions than against trusts.

The preamble of the Populist platform in 1892 asserted that

"The fruits of the toil of millions are boldly stolen to build up colossal fortunes for a few, unprecedented in the history of mankind; and the possessors of these in turn despise the Republic and endanger liberty. From the same prolific womb of governmental injustice we breed the two great classes—tramps and millionaires."

Meanwhile the two great political parties

"propose to drown the outcries of a plundered people with the uproar of a sham battle over the tariff . . . to sacrifice our homes, lives and children on the altar of mammon."

As remedy the Populists proposed, in the economic sphere, free and unlimited coinage of silver, low interest rates, abolition of the national banks, a graduated income tax, public ownership of railways; in the social sphere, legislation to protect the rights of labour and to shorten hours; in the political sphere, electoral reform, the initiative and referendum and the direct election of Senators. Their Presidential candidate, J. B. Weaver, obtained over 1 million votes, the largest number given to a genuinely third-party candidate between 1860 and 1920—in 1912 the three candidates really only represented two parties. The position of the Populists in American history is strangely like that of the Chartists in our own, in that although at the time they failed to secure their aims, yet their programme remained as the blueprint for subsequent reformers, and most of its proposals—free silver, the public ownership of railroads and a limitation of the Presidency to a single term being the main exceptions—ultimately found a place either in State or in Federal legislation.

Urban workers too were organising during this period and starting anew their political education. In 1866 an attempt was made to federate individual trade unions in a National Labor Union, but this attempt failed, and in 1872 the Union was succeeded by the Noble Order of the Knights of Labor, organised in 1869 in Philadelphia by the garment workers. As befitting its city of origin, the Order aimed at a brotherly union of skilled and unskilled workers without distinction of trade, and also of capitalists, merchants and farmers. Its great days came with Terence V. Powderley, appointed Grand Master in 1878. Although the Order advocated the substitution of arbitration for strikes, it yet pursued an aggressive policy and in 1884 scored a notable success in a railroad strike which forced the formidable Jay

Gould to negotiate. In these years it grew rapidly, and in 1886, when it called another railway strike, it had 700,000 members. This strike, however, failed, and a further succession of failures, coupled with the difficulty of holding skilled and unskilled workers together, led to the gradual collapse of the Order. Its place was taken by the American Federation of Labor, a national federation of self-governing trade unions founded originally in 1881, but re-organised in 1886 by Samuel Gompers. Gompers was President of the Federation almost uninterruptedly from 1882 till his death in 1924, and more than any other single man was responsible for the non-political character of American trade unionism.

At this period American trade unions were distinguished by two characteristic features. First, they were organised on a craft basis and excluded the unskilled workers who were to form a gradually increasing proportion of the American working class. Second, they accepted the capitalist system and concentrated on the purely economic organisation of wage-earners for collective bargaining and control of job opportunities, so as to guarantee employment to their members.

That labour organisation should intensify was inevitable once the closure of the frontier ended the possibility of agriculture as an alternative field of employment, so that industry was flooded with immigrants, threatening established wage standards. That organisation should be on a craft basis was probably also inevitable, given that these immigrants were men of little or no education and speaking various tongues, so that it was not easy to find any common ground except that of craftsmanship. When that was lacking, there was little to bring the workers together and bridge the gulf of language, and, moreover, to the unskilled, no union could guarantee employment, even if his wages had been sufficient to support a union on the scale to which organisers were becoming accustomed. If we add that at this time America was still regarded as a land of opportunity, so that all workers expected soon to be at least independent workmen, if not employers themselves, the wonder is that trade unionism progressed as far as it did.

These characteristics of American unionism determined the function of the American Federation of Labor as Gompers saw it, which was to ensure that the various craft unions did not encroach on one another's jurisdiction and to maintain a national lobby at Washington just as State and City Federations maintained lobbies or representatives at State capitals and municipal offices. Only in relatively rare emergencies did the Federation envisage any alliance between workers as workers. The organisation of the unskilled had to wait for half a century, marked by the rise and fall of the Industrial Workers of the World between 1904 and 1918, who combined socialism with an aggressive unionism on an industrial instead of a craft basis. By 1900 the membership of the American Federation of Labor was over a half a million, and it reached the 2 million mark by 1920.

As the unions grew in strength, strikes grew in intensity and became matters of public concern and often of Federal intervention. Here we can only mention the most important. In 1892 occurred the great strike in Andrew Carnegie's Homestead works for an increase in the wage scale. From the national point of view this strike, and others of the same year with the same object, showed that tariff protection was not ensuring the high wages which its advocates claimed would follow. That the strike should have been broken by armed Pinkerton detectives and State militia gave a shock to nascent Liberal opinion, which found its echo in one of the resolutions of the Populist platform. The effect of the defeat was to keep the steel industry substantially free of unionism for nearly forty years.

Among the numerous disturbances that followed the panic of 1893 should be noted the strike of 1894 of the American Railway Union, led by Eugene V. Debs against the Pullman Car Company because of its refusal to discuss grievances, a strike which tied up traffic throughout the North. President Cleveland supported the railway owners, and when Altgeld, the Governor of Illinois, refused to ask for the help of Federal troops sent them on his own initiative, claiming a constitutional right to do so; Altgeld's protest was ignored and the strike was smashed.

The Pullman strike is important on various grounds. Firstly, Cleveland's action was "a new and imposing development of national sovereignty," a self-conscious display of the national power which was at the same time exhibiting itself in foreign wars and the acquisition of colonies. Secondly, business men learned that "the jurisdiction of courts to interfere in such matters by injunction is one recognised from ancient times by indubitable authority." Thereafter injunctions were freely employed in industrial disputes until Wilson's Presidency, when their use was for a time forbidden by the Clayton Act. Finally, the legal history of the strike drove home to workers everywhere the truth that the constitutional provisions of the Fourteenth Amendment designed to protect the individual were being turned by judicial decisions into instruments whereby he became the more completely enslaved to the big corporation.

Anger at what appeared to be judicial perversions of the intentions of the Legislature plus the strikes of 1894 plus unemployed hunger-marchers plus the Senate's action over the Wilson-Gorman tariff plus the Supreme Court's veto of the income tax all boiled up to convert the 1896 election struggle from a technical and fiscal issue between gold and free silver into a social conflict between the "elephant pluto-crats," Wall Street and the Republican party on one side and on the other the "Eagles of the West" and South, the producing masses of the nation menaced by the new slavery. Bryan's great speech at the Democratic Convention with its famous peroration, "you shall not crucify mankind upon a Cross of Gold," not only attacked the Republican programme, but also drew a class and sectional distinction between farmers and miners on one hand and on the other the "few financial magnates who in a back room corner the money of the world." He called for a new Andrew Jackson, "to stand as Jackson did against the encroachment of organised wealth." The final voting showed the cotton, prairie and silver States arrayed against the industrial and old grain States. The election has been summed up as

"not only the last protest of the old agrarian order against industrialism, it was also the first attempt of the new order to clean house. Bryan was the bridge between Andrew Jackson and Franklin D. Roosevelt."

In 1896, as in 1932, it could be said,

"There are those who believe that if you will only legislate to make the well-to-do prosperous, their prosperity will leak through on those below. The Democratic idea, however, has been that if you make the masses prosperous, their prosperity will find its way through every class which rests upon them."

In the defeat of Bryan, the American people registered their decision to accept a capitalist and Hamiltonian system, and their attention was then distracted from domestic and social problems by a period of prosperity and colonial expansion. The interval till the Presidency of Theodore Roosevelt is bridged by the activities of the "muckrakers," the continuance of social legislation within the States and the growth of "Progressivism."

The term "muckrakers" was applied by Theodore Roosevelt in 1906 to those writers who were vigorous during his Presidency in exposing economic, social and political abuses. The literary protest against plutocracy had started at least twenty-five years earlier with such books as Henry George's *Progress and Poverty* (1880), which achieved international fame and influence, and Edward Bellamy's *Looking Backward* (1888). In 1899 Thorstein Veblen wrote his *Economic Theory of the Leisure Class,* a shrewd and sardonic attack upon the economic inequalities of the "Gilded Age" and its practice of "conspicuous waste."

These writers, however, worked on a high plane of argument. The muckrakers—journalists, magazine writers and novelists—got down to ground-level, explored the back alleys, gutters and even sewers of contemporary society, faithfully reported what they found and named the individuals they held responsible. The methods of the great industrial combinations were unveiled in such books as Ida Tarbell's *History of the Standard Oil Company* (1904) and Upton Sinclair's *The Jungle* (1906), dealing with the insanitary conditions in the Chicago packing houses run by the Beef Trust; Jake Riis, in *How the other Half Lives* (1890), dealt with housing conditions in New York, and in a classic series of articles in *McClure's Magazine,* later published as *The Shame of the Cities,* Lincoln Steffens floodlit the political corruption of cities and municipalities. Such revelations came as a severe shock and caused an increasing realisation of the threat that was developing to the "American Dream," socially, economically and politically.

The term "Progressive Movement" is that applied to the general movement of reform growing out of the discontent which the muckrakers fed with facts. The Progressives aimed at making government, Municipal, State or National, both more democratic and more efficient. Some reforms were achieved, but often the reformers proved less competent administrators than the corrupt practitioners whom they had expelled or else the mere effort to clean house exhausted their energies, so that the old gang simply returned to a house swept and garnished. Pressure for reform of the Civil Service flowed naturally from the demand for reform in Municipal administration.

Demand for social legislation and the reform of labour conditions was also intensified as a result of the muckrakers' revelations. Laws regulating hours of work had been passed in several States in the sixties and seventies, but their effect, as of those prohibiting child labour, had been more apparent than real. Indeed, as industry spread through the South after 1890, the general picture became worse rather than better. Moreover, such legislation was always liable to be invalidated by judicial decisions as being contrary to the principles of freedom of property and contract as embodied in the Fifth and Fourteenth Amendments to the Constitution. In the Jacobs case of 1885 the New York Court of Appeals disallowed an Act designed to prevent cigar-making in tenement houses, a decision which revealed the judges as being equally ignorant of cigar-making and tenement houses. It was this decision which gave Theodore Roosevelt, who had been a member of the Legislature which passed the Act, his first revelation of judicial obstruction of necessary reform.

Nevertheless, gradually progress was registered. A dissenting judgment of Mr. Justice Holmes in 1905 declared roundly that

"The case is decided upon an economic theory which a large part of the country does not entertain. . . . The Fourteenth Amendment does not enact Mr. Herbert Spencer's Social Statics,"

and the Supreme Court gradually changed its views.

If the share of the people in government was to be increased, political reforms too were necessary, and these also were first tried out in the States. They included the nomination of political candidates for office by the people themselves in "direct primaries" instead of by boss-ridden conventions, the "initiative," whereby the people could demand and initiate legislation, the "referendum" to approve or reject legislation by direct popular vote, and the "recall" of public officials. On the national level the direct popular election of Senators was demanded.

The first State to adopt a direct primary law was Wisconsin, in 1903, where "Fighting Bob" LaFollette was making the State a proving-ground for new ideas worked out in the State University and the Legislative Reference Library, which became, under Charles McCarthy, an invaluable political research laboratory. Within the next four years seven other States followed suit. The initiative and referendum were first introduced into a State constitution by South Dakota in 1898, and similar provisions for direct legislation are now found in some form or other in nearly half the States. The principle of the recall—the right to force a referendum on the continuance in office of any public official, including judges, and first instituted in Los Angeles in 1903—was also adopted by Oregon in 1908. This too has now been adopted by a dozen States.

But none of these devices has as yet been adopted nationally, although Theodore Roosevelt in 1912 advocated a variation of the recall which McCarthy had suggested, whereby it should apply less to the judges themselves than to their decisions, since "every public servant . . . at times makes mistakes. . . . But when a judge decides a constitutional question . . . the people should have the right to recall that decision if they think it wrong." The popular influence in the direct primary was gradually nullified as professional politicians perfected their technique of political control, while the other devices have not yielded significant results. Considering the actual use made of them, not only in the United States but elsewhere, we may well question whether democracy can be produced by machinery.

The demand for popular election of Senators instead of by the State legislatures originated in the Populist programme, but the necessary constitutional amendment was steadily blocked by the Senate. Starting, however, with Nevada in 1899, various States passed laws binding their legislatures to elect candidates endorsed in a State primary election, and by 1912 some thirty States had passed legislation of this kind. The Seventeenth Amendment of 1913, which wrote direct election into the Constitution while merely registering what was, in effect, an accomplished fact, did at the same time mark a real advance in American political democracy, for it broke down one of the barriers to popular government on which the Founding Fathers had most relied.

The Progressive party was filled with hope and the conservative interests were equally dismayed when Theodore Roosevelt—"that damned cowboy," as Mark Hanna bitterly ejaculated—unexpectedly succeeded to the Presidency. Like Bryan and Wilson, he was a moralist and crusader for righteousness, and he shared Bryan's enormous human sympathy. Unlike Wilson, however, his perceptions were emotional rather than intellectual. When he succeeded McKinley he found himself the titular head of a party which had secured power with a mandate to let business alone. Yet his progressive instincts and his sense of what the ordinary citizen demanded urged him along the path of reform. His attitude to Trusts expressed in his first Annual Message to Congress reflected clearly the unhappy dilemma of the American when faced with big business.

"There have been abuses connected with the accumulation of wealth. . . . The captains of industry . . . have on the whole done great good to our people. . . . Moreover, we should recognise the immense importance of this material development by leaving as unhampered as is compatible with the public good the strong and forceful men upon whom the success of business operations inevitably rests."

He tried to differentiate between the use and abuse of corporations and to give the Americans the best of both worlds, to leave the organisation of business sufficiently free to ensure prosperity, but sufficiently under control to prevent the complete transformation of the country from a democracy to a plutocracy.

"Th' thrusts," commented Mr. Dooley, "are heejous monsthers built up by the inlightened intherprise ov th' men that have done so much to advance progress in our beloved counthry. On wan hand I wud stamp them undher fut, on th' other hand, not so fast."

Roosevelt recommended the establishment of a Department of Commerce, which was set up in 1903 and a Bureau of Corporations to investigate trusts and provide material for prosecutions. While Harrison, Cleveland and McKinley between them had launched only eighteen prosecutions under the Sherman Act, Roosevelt launched 44, beginning with a case against the Northern Securities Company, whereby a potentially widespreading movement of railway consolidation was checked.

The most dramatic episode of Roosevelt's first term was his forcible settlements of the strike of 1902 in the anthracite coal fields by threatening to take over the mines unless the owners would agree to submit the dispute to arbitration. The arbitral board which he then appointed gave the workers a shorter working day of 8–9 hours and a 10 per cent. rise in pay against their demand for a 20 per cent. increase, and also recognised their union. This was the last successful coal strike until the era of John L. Lewis, who in 1902 was a twenty-one-year-old mule-driver in the western coalfields.

But neither his first nor his second term was remarkable in the field of social legislation. He supported legislation for the reduction of working hours, and had Congress enact laws establishing workman's compensation for government employees and prohibiting child labour in the District of Columbia. But he gave no support to national legislation against child labour, and though in a message to Congress in 1907 he ascribed the financial panic of that year to "speculative folly of a few men of great wealth," he went no farther than to complain of the failure of the laws to enforce upon owners of property their duty to the public.

Since it is perhaps merely a vain assumption that the cure for ineffective legislation is more legislation, it is doubtless to Theodore Roosevelt's credit that he pegged away with what he had and continued to prosecute successfully under the Sherman Act. But it cannot have escaped his notice that the defeated combinations regularly reintegrated. In 1911 the Supreme Court in the Standard Oil case again modified its views and held that only those combinations were illegal which unduly restrained commerce. Mr. Justice Harlan, who had written the Northern Securities judgment, vigorously dissented, but the majority decision was in line with Roosevelt's own view that there were good and bad trusts, of which the latter abused their power and must be dissolved, while the former gave the country the benefits of size and community of interest and should be encouraged. The New Deal of his cousin, Franklin, was to exhibit in some respects a similar philosophy.

The most original achievement of Theodore Roosevelt's Presidency and his most valuable contribution to American life was his inauguration of the principle of conservation of natural resources as a national aim. He set aside 150 million acres under the Forest Reserve Act of

1891, and another 85 million in Alaska and the North-west, until their mineral and water resources had been studied. Irrigation of arid western States was facilitated by the Newlands Act of 1902, which provided funds for this purpose from the sale of public lands. In 1907 a National Conservation Conference was held at the White House. Unhappily public interest in the subject depended entirely on Roosevelt's personal drive. After he left the White House activity declined until 1932, when the Newlands Act became the basis of a Federal policy of dam building and the recommendations of his Conference found a concrete expression in the Tennessee Valley Authority.

At the conclusion of his second term Theodore Roosevelt—the first Vice-President ever to be elected President—presented William Howard Taft to the Republican party as his successor and, after seeing him installed in the White House, left the country, partly so as not to embarrass Taft, and partly to enjoy the delights of foreign travel and big-game hunting. Taft was at heart a mild constitutional lawyer, and almost immediately got into trouble over the tariff, of which a revision was now demanded by the mid-West grain-growing States, ever the main supporters of the Progressive movement.

Taft in his Inaugural Address had proposed that the tariff should be reduced to the difference between home and foreign costs of production, and that any loss of revenue should be met by an inheritance tax. But he had not the vigour of his predecessor, and believed that the President's power was restricted to what the Constitution permitted. This may have been good constitutional law, but was definitely bad political practice, since it gave the political initiative to Congress, which was then controlled by the Old Guard of the Republican party. The result was the Payne-Aldrich Bill of 1909, in which the majority of changes were upwards. Taft, however, called the tariff "the best the country ever had" and signed the Bill, thereby alienating the Progressive Republicans. At the Congressional election of 1910 the Progressives increased their strength in both houses of Congress and some Eastern States normally Republican elected Democratic Governors, among whom was Woodrow Wilson in New Jersey.

In an attempt to retrieve the situation Taft tried to get a reciprocal trade pact with Canada whereby duties on Canadian raw materials and foodstuffs should be reduced in return for a lowering of Canadian duties on farm implements and other machinery. Since the American import duties on machinery were left untouched, the Eastern Republicans supported the scheme, but the Middle and Far West timber and farming interests attacked it through fear of Canadian competition. The Democrats, in a rare burst of political shrewdness, supported the scheme, since it was so evidently splitting the Republicans, and with their help it passed Congress in 1911, only to be rejected by the Canadians.

Despite this setback, Taft was renominated as the Republican candidate for the Presidential election of 1912 on a conservative programme. Theodore Roosevelt was nominated by the Progressive wing of the Republicans, known as the "Bull Moose" party, from the animal to which their candidate, in a moment of exuberance, had compared himself. He was now advocating the "Square Deal"—economic democracy with greater equality of opportunity and of reward, the right of the community to regulate private wealth—together with the political measures advocated by the Populists, which he had hitherto either ignored or opposed. Such a programme was far too Radical to attract a majority of Republican voters, while the Southerners who might have rallied to him were also alienated by his having invited Booker T. Washington, an eminent negro, to the White House. The result of the election campaign was disastrous to the Republican Party, and not merely in a purely political sense. Indeed, the fact that the split ensured the election of Wilson was perhaps less important than the fact that it killed the Progressive movement in the party and ended any hope of liberalising it for at least a generation. Convinced that Progressivism, like pioneering, did not pay, the party retired upon its Conservative wing and for the next thirty years maintained an uncompromising hostility to Liberal principles.

What had the Progressive Movement expected from Theodore Roosevelt and Taft, and what had it received? Undoubtedly it expected that some at least of its aims should be written into national legislation and into the Constitution. This it did not obtain from Roosevelt. His importance did not lie in legislation, but in the fact that he dramatised the issues and that, on the whole, he asked the right questions even if he failed to find the right answers. He saw what was the fact, that there were potentialities for good as well as for evil in large aggregates of business and believed that trusts needed regulation rather than dissolution. He contributed also the example of a President who, for the first time since Andrew Johnson, both could and did take from Congress their political initiative and exercise it himself. For this reason it is the more regrettable that he failed to get any regulatory legislation through Congress. Though he denounced "malefactors of great wealth," he took no steps to curb individual fortunes or secure by taxation a more equitable distribution of wealth. Though hailed as the greatest Republican President since Lincoln, he was, in fact, too "regular" a politician to be a successful reformer, for he was always ready to compromise rather than split the party, and he avoided really controversial issues, like the level of tariffs or reform of the banking system.

His attacks on Taft were therefore particularly undeserved, since Taft had at least grasped the nettle of tariff reform, even if he plucked no flowers from it. As a trust-buster Taft launched more prosecutions than Theodore Roosevelt, he strengthened the Interstate Commerce Commission, limited election expenses and made a valuable administrative separation of the Department of Labor from that of Commerce, thus paving the way for the establishment of the former in 1913 as one of Cabinet rank. He was also responsible for setting up in the Department of Labor the Children's Bureau, under Julia Lathrop, of Hull House, to protect and improve the status of children. The Sixteenth and Seventeenth Amendments should also be chalked up to his credit, for although not ratified till 1913, they were passed by Congress in 1909 and 1912 respectively. The passage of the Sixteenth, which made possible a Federal Income Tax, was important as a fiscal measure, but also from the social point of view because the taxing machinery provided for the first time a national review of individual incomes which was published, so that the nation could identify its men of great wealth and decide whether or not they were malefactors. The

Seventeenth, establishing direct election of Senators, swept away the last constitutional safeguard against political democracy. Both had figured in the Populist programme.

Taft, though more conservative than Theodore Roosevelt, did not betray the Progressive cause nor entirely fail to continue its policies. But there was a failure in both the Republican Presidents which went to the root of the matter, a failure to perceive that more was required to safeguard democracy and the "American dream" than a few reforms in the superstructure of an edifice which was fundamentally sound. It was the foundations themselves which required testing, and perhaps reconstructing. In 1913 came the turn of Wilson and the Democrats.

PART II

Woodrow Wilson : from Prospect to the White House

Chapter Four

" Princeton in the Nation's Service "

THE years between Wilson's return to Princeton as Professor of Political Jurisprudence and his election to the White House are interesting as showing both how his own views developed, and how during the years following Colonel Harvey's dramatic speech of 1906 his position as the rising hope of the Democratic Party became established.

When Wilson became Professor in 1890, Princeton had already begun to change from the old-fashioned College of New Jersey, at which he had been a student. The College, fourth oldest in the U.S.A. after Harvard, William and Mary, and Yale, had been founded in 1746 by a band of ascetic Presbyterians who in a monastic atmosphere and with infinitesimal financial endowment started to teach "Latin, Greek, a little mathematics and a wealth of Scotch theology." Under Witherspoon, a "fighting parson," it played an historical part in the American Revolutionary War—one of its trophies being a captured English cannon; in 1780 the

Continental Congress met there, and it was from Princeton that George Washington sent his Farewell Address to the army.

These associations had a strong appeal for Wilson's historical and traditionalist outlook, as had also the atmosphere of prayer and religious devotion which still remained in 1890, although worldly influences were growing. The old austerity gave way to easier living as the country's rising wealth was reflected in new buildings and especially in the eating clubs, which at Princeton took the place of the Greek-letter Fraternities of other Colleges. Under President Patton Princeton became essentially a rich man's college—"a delightfully aristocratic place"—with declining standards of scholarship, typified in the classic tale of an indignant student's comment on an examination paper, "This question is unfair; it requires thought." Wilson was the son of one of the poor and austere students of earlier days who had attended prayers at 5 a.m. and chopped firewood in the intervals of study. To him the purpose of attending college was not to join fraternities or clubs, and have a good time, but to study the world and prepare to work in it.

These views were not yet obvious when President Patton appointed him. But Wilson, who early established his reputation with the students as a teacher, soon also became the leader of the younger members of the Faculty at a time when College Presidents were not the autocrats they later became and professors had a substantial share in managing their institutions. As might be expected, his influence was on the side of the humanities rather than of science. For the next dozen years he devoted himself to the duties of his professorship and to the writing of history. He lived comfortably, though not lavishly, in a house full of his in-laws, one of whom has written, "He loved gay nonsense. He could play the fool enchantingly." A favourite entertainment of his was to imitate a Fourth of July orator who gesticulated with his legs instead of with his arms. He also—and this was unusual among contemporary faculty members—knew the local inhabitants and tradesmen, thereby showing a lack of exclusiveness which was to stand him in good stead in his political campaigns. In his own circle he was one of the leaders in a band devoted to good talk. He made several visits to England, notably in 1896 and 1899, covering a good deal of ground, particularly in the Lake District, on a bicycle, being an "experienced wheeler" in the days when cycling was an art and not just a means of locomotion. He visited Cambridge to see Maitland, the historian, and also went to Oxford, and from both Universities he drew ideas for Princeton, though commenting, "I am a better American for having been there."

In 1896 Wilson was chosen to deliver an

address at the commemoration of the one hundred and fiftieth anniversary of the foundation of the College, on which occasion its name was changed to the University of Princeton. He chose for his theme "Princeton in the Nation's Service," and in what proved to be the outstanding address of the celebration reviewed the College's contribution to American society and national life and urged that in the future the University should not hold aloof, but use its influence "not to change but to strengthen society" and to raise up leaders for the nation. He also made an eloquent plea for a liberal education as a means of avoiding the revolutionary agitation likely to spring from the spirit of experiment and contempt for the past that was bred by science. A liberal education kept society balanced by tradition while not opposing genuine progress. By this address he was marked out as the inevitable successor to President Patton.

The President of an American University holds a higher place and enjoys greater prestige than the head of an English or Scots University. Not only are his powers greater over the University itself, but he is often a leading figure in the State and even in the nation. When, on June 9th, 1902, the Trustees of the University elected him to the Presidency, Wilson had yet to reach this stature, but he was ripe for the post, had completed his studies of American history and politics and was ready to tackle educational and other problems on the widest scale. Princeton, situated between the North and the South, was a singularly effective platform for the exposition of his views. Moreover, a post which possessed both power and initiative, with no checks and balances and where a failure of leadership produced not a constitutional deadlock but a change of leader, answered Wilson's main concept in the field of government—namely that of "responsible leadership." Looking at the University as a State in miniature, he wrote to his wife that he was content, for he felt like a Prime Minister. That he was not unconscious of the opportunity for leadership in a wider field was shown in a phrase in his Inaugural Address on October 26th, 1902: "A new age is before us in which, it would seem, we must lead the world."

Wilson's problem was to improve the standard of work and bring some unity of thought and purpose into the University without alienating conservative professors or wealthy alumni. Already, as a Faculty member, he had been largely responsible for introducing the student honour system, whereby invigilation at examinations was abolished and the students signed an undertaking on their honour that they had not cheated. Now he turned to the examinations themselves, making them more rigorous and requiring students who failed to leave the University. In this he carried opinion with him

and even induced the Trustees to contemplate
almost with satisfaction a fall in numbers, which
he rightly assured them would only be temporary and produce a great improvement in quality.
Still in pursuit of intellectual unity, he revised
the curriculum, in which students had previously
had free choice of subject, so that during their
first two years they were restricted to groups of
subjects having some internal harmony.

His next venture was more ambitious. President Garfield had once given his idea of a
liberal education as "a log in the woods with a
boy at one end and Mark Hopkins at the other,"
and Wilson was equally convinced that the
truest and best education proceeded from the
free play of mind on mind in simple surroundings. He desired, therefore, to increase the number of Princeton instructors, and proposed
further that they should live among the students,
in "dormitories" built for the purpose, so as to
be always available for discourse and advice and
not merely during formal periods of joint study.
The "Preceptorial System," as it was called,
resembled somewhat the Oxford tutorial system
as he had seen it on his travels. Wilson's scheme,
with the buildings it implied and the creation
of a Graduate School which had been mooted in
1896 but had made little subsequent progress,
was estimated to require an endowment of 12
million dollars. With irresistible audacity he
asked for this sum to be subscribed, and enough

was immediately raised to enable the required number of new tutors to start in the autumn of 1905, to be duly hailed by the student body:

> *"Here's to these Preceptor guys*
> *Fifty stiffs to make us wise."*

To Wilson, the weakness of the English system was its life tenure, which permitted the teachers to go to seed. He proposed a maximum tenure of five years. The short term proved no deterrent, and he had no difficulty in recruiting his team, many of whom later achieved great distinction, though generally and inevitably elsewhere than at Princeton.

The institution of Preceptors marks the end of Wilson's first four years as President, years of spontaneous drive backed by public idealism, during which he achieved undeniable success in improving Princeton's education on its technical side by methods that were later copied elsewhere. Thereafter his purpose grew to raise the spirit of Princeton, and with it grew opposition. Already a dangerous situation was being created, for while Princeton certainly benefited by the gifts which Wilson elicited from wealthy Americans (for example Andrew Carnegie, whose gift of a lake when Wilson really wanted buildings brought the neat acknowledgment, "Mr. Carnegie, we need bread, and you have given us cake"), yet at the same time the dependency of the University on such gifts was made manifest and the time might come when the donors might doubt the wisdom of the changes in the old aristocratic atmosphere that were implicit in Wilson's reforms and even feel that the influence of wealth should be decisive over that of the President of the University. After all, this was the era of Dollar Diplomacy. The contest came over the proposal to substitute Quadrangles for the Clubs and over the location of the Graduate School.

The erection of Dormitories, where bodies of students and teachers should live together in place of the Clubs whose luxury and exclusiveness had been steadily increasing, was, as we have seen, an essential part of Wilson's Preceptorial System and had been accepted by the Trustees as a technical reform. But the change was also essential, in Wilson's view, on the social side, if Princeton was to play its part in training leaders for the nation's service. For the dangers which threatened the national democratic tradition could not be adequately met, or indeed met at all, by people whose training had taken place among undemocratic surroundings of luxury and privilege. By the time Wilson became President of the University, membership of a Club rather than the acquisition of knowledge, social rather than academic distinction, had become the aim of the typical Princeton student. If he failed to win election to a Club during "Bicker Week," he was apt to regard his College career as a complete failure. In Wilson's expressive phrase, "the sideshows have swallowed up the circus." The position was not peculiar to Princeton alone; it existed at Harvard and Wisconsin, and at Columbia C. F. Adams agreed with Wilson's diagnosis and advocated a similar remedy. Wilson therefore regarded himself as dealing with a problem of fundamental significance, not merely for university education, but for the whole American way of life. In 1907 he proposed that in place of the Clubs there should be erected Halls of Residence or Quadrangles. In June the Trustees accepted the plan, but during the summer it came under hot fire from both Club members and alumni, who asserted that the compulsory mingling of all sorts and conditions of students infringed the right of every man to choose his companions. Threats to withdraw financial support were widely made, and in face of such strong feeling the Trustees in October withdrew their acceptance of the plan.

If Wilson's decision to abandon the practice of law for the study of politics may be taken as the first milestone in his career, this decision by the Princeton Trustees may be taken as the second, for, among other consequences, it made him consider more seriously the suggestion that he should abandon the study of politics for its practice. For to Wilson the struggle over the Quadrangles was one between vested interests and social privilege on the one hand and intellectual vitality and social equality on the other, and thus a reflection of the problems vexing the nation at large whose solution he held to be impossible in a country lacking positive leadership. The action of the Trustees he regarded as defending an undemocratic way of life at Princeton and thus paralleling the action of those forces in the nation which were socially and politically dangerous. The success of his plan would not only have greatly influenced American education, but would also have been a first step towards restoring the reality of the American Dream, now so grievously threatened. Wilson decided to make one more attempt to achieve this success by appealing to the bar of public opinion, which he was confident would support him when sufficiently informed of the issues at stake. He therefore addressed meetings of alumni in various parts of the country and found that, while the Easterners remained obdurate in opposition, Westerners supported him, a sectional cleavage which followed the same lines on the political issues of American democracy being posed at the same time by William Jennings Bryan.

This was Wilson's first practical lesson in how men act under pressure. His technique of appealing to the people, and the philosophy behind it, foreshadow the course he followed at certain critical moments when President of the United States. That his campaign was overshadowed by ill-health was also not without significance, though its failure was also partly due to the Quadrangle question becoming swamped in the controversy over the Graduate College, with which indeed Wilson himself linked it by his insistence on the need for the integration of all University activities for the supreme purpose of inculcating intellectual discipline. Meanwhile the public controversy his action aroused, resentment at the picture he revealed of cliques and aristocracy and idleness in the midst of a hard-working and theoretically class-less democracy, together with his own personal appearances, laid the foundation of the popular support which he was to receive on his formal entry into political life.

The struggle over the situation of the Graduate College went back to 1896, when Andrew West was made Dean of the proposed school, with instructions to explore its possibilities and to report direct to the Trustees, thus giving him a measure of independence of the President of the University which might ultimately become rivalry. In his Inaugural Address of 1902 Wilson urged that it be located within the existing University boundaries—"to stimulate and set the pace for the whole University." But little progress was made in the next half-dozen years, and as Wilson became increasingly immersed in his plans for the reform of the social atmosphere of the University, Dean

West's attitude sharpened into antagonism and the question became a personal issue between the two men, with West now advocating a site remote from the University campus, as if to emphasise the independence of the College and of his authority. None the less, in 1908 Wilson persuaded the Trustees to adopt a site on the Campus. West countered with an offer of $500,000 received from William C. Procter, a soap manufacturer of Cincinnati, on condition that the College be sited in accordance with West's wishes and that Princeton itself raise a further half-million. This last would not have been difficult. Wilson was both piqued and alarmed, because the proposal not only involved the disintegration of the University as he conceived it, but if accepted on Procter's terms would demonstrate again the dangerous power of wealth. He therefore persuaded the Trustees to decline the gift.

The unprecedented spectacle of a University refusing the chance of a million dollars astounded the country, dramatised the problem of the proper place of wealth in a democracy and increased the national interest in and curiosity about the man who could persuade a University to so strange a course. In May, however, a Massachusetts manufacturer, Isaac Wyman, died and in his will left to the Graduate College, with West as trustee, a sum first computed as 10 million dollars; Procter simultaneously renewed his offer. Although the Wyman legacy ultimately turned out to be only 2 million dollars, the battle was lost. To secure the rejection of even the lesser sum was beyond Wilson's powers. In June it was accepted and the Graduate College was in due course erected on a site a mile or more from that desired by Wilson. On September 15th Wilson was nominated Democratic candidate for the Governorship of New Jersey and promptly resigned from the Presidency of the University.

He was succeeded by J. G. Hibben, one of his oldest friends, whom he had nevertheless implacably discarded when Hibben finally joined the opposition to his Quadrangle scheme. This election was the final drop in Wilson's cup of bitterness, and he refused to attend Hibben's inauguration, although as Governor of the State he had an official obligation to do so, nor ever resumed his friendship. Nevertheless, Hibben was a sound choice after the excitements of Wilson's regime. In 1924 he appointed a committee to consider the problems of the Clubs, whose report was a complete vindication of Wilson's views. But Princeton still awaits its Quadrangles or any visible monument to the best known of its Presidents.

Yet although Wilson had to quit the field, his career at Princeton cannot be written off as a failure. It is true that he did not succeed in achieving the full measure of his plans, but his was the impetus which started Princeton on the road towards its present and universally acknowledged high place in American scholarship. And for Wilson himself, his twenty years at Princeton were invaluable. As an historian he had some understanding of the origins of America and the forces which were moulding the nation. But this was book knowledge only. The journeys he made during his Presidency and his lectures and speeches, first to academic and then to popular audiences, gave him a widened and first-hand knowledge of his own country. He learnt "how unlike the United States" was New England besides winning, as has already been mentioned, a countrywide body of supporters ready for his entry into national politics.

At the same time, however, during his tenure of Prospect—the official residence of the President of Princeton—he became less accessible than when he lived in Library Place, so that there grew up the belief that he was by nature personally cold and aloof. Aloofness, indeed, was forced upon him and strict regulation of his time and energy as a means of safeguarding his health, which was never strong; for the same reason he had to abandon sociable games of billiards at the Faculty Club so as to avoid the inevitable member who wished to canvass him, informally, of course, on some business which might easily have waited till the morrow. Being thus thrown back on the resources of his own household, it was certainly unfortunate that that household consisted entirely of women—his wife, sister-in-law, three daughters and a cousin, who all adored him. His brother-in-law, Stockton Axson, did not move with the family from Library Place to Prospect, and Wilson missed the mental stimulus and questioning that would have been provided by the continuation of his earlier conversational circle or by a vigorous son of his own. In truth he became a somewhat lonely man, so that all his decisions had to be personal ones. Thus his belief in personal responsibility was reinforced and he tended increasingly not merely to rely on his own judgment—which in a leader is a good trait—but to believe in its infallibility—which in any circumstances is not.

The period of his University Presidency marks also a significant change in his political thought. The basic themes are set out in his earliest essay on politics, *Cabinet Government in the United States,* published in 1879, and are more fully worked out in subsequent volumes, notably *Congressional Government* (1885), *The State* (1889) and *Constitutional Government in the United States* (1908). Wilson recognised that the machinery whereby the American Constitution carried into effect the doctrine of the separation of powers produced, in fact, their isolation and made strict observance of the Constitution the surest guarantee that no action would ever be taken to disrupt the social and political structure established by the Founding Fathers who had succeeded—uniquely in history —in stopping a revolution at the point most convenient to the class which started it. Because of this isolation of President, Congress and Supreme Court—because, to quote a later writer, "A Senator outlives a President, a President outlives a Representative and the Judges of the Supreme Court outlive all"— political leadership fell into the hands of the Congressional Committees which met in secret under dictatorial chairmen. In Wilson's view a simple political reform of almost a mechanical nature would suffice to counteract the low state of American politics—namely the assumption by the President of executive leadership in government together with a responsible Cabinet system on the English model.

But since he wanted to save the system of government as by the Constitution established, he did not draw the obvious conclusion from his study—namely that if responsibility in politics is necessary, then the Constitution must go, since the object of its checks and balances was to prevent the focusing of responsibility, to prevent things being done rather than to promote action. In 1893, in the second Cleveland administration, he urged the President, now that a Democratic majority in Congress united the Legislative and Executive elements of the government, to

98

resume the leadership which had been lacking in American politics since the time of Lincoln. But neither Cleveland nor Wilson himself in his professorial days perceived that economic democracy is an essential of political democracy or that the strict observance of the Constitution as a guarantee of the status quo was as essential to the newly arisen industrial interests of the North as it had been in 1860 to the great planters of the South. Wilson, whose interests were always more in the machinery and functions of government than in economics as such —the creation and distribution of wealth and the mechanism of the market—did not doubt the goodness of contemporary economic institutions. Anything bad was the result of individual criminal conduct or ignorance, not of the system itself. Hence the way to remedy the admitted evils of political corruption, poverty, illiteracy and bad social conditions generally was to promote the moral welfare of the masses and to prepare the best minds of the educated classes for public service.

His book *Constitutional Government in the United States,* published while President of Princeton, represented his mature thought on this subject. The criticism of government by congressional committees is repeated, but the tone of moderate conservatism is even more marked than in the earlier volume. He showed how the existence of secret committees militates against good government, but hardly touched on the corruption which goes with secrecy. He may be said to describe rather than to condemn. He seemed to regard the U.S. Constitution as a Newtonian system which, once started, would and should never cease to function and in which slow and gradual changes can alone be expected. Nine years earlier, in *The State*, he had written, "In politics nothing radically novel may safely be attempted."

Thus while he was eloquent on the need for reform he differed from the muckrakers and Progressives on every point of policy. He might castigate big business, but such mild governmental interference as he had advocated in his professorial lectures had now given place to a doctrine of reliance on the enlightened individual. It is thus easy to see why in 1906 he appeared to the representatives of business and finance gathered at the Lotos Club as an equally eloquent but far safer Presidential candidate for the Democratic party than W. J. Bryan. His political views were soundly Conservative, and it was reasonable to doubt whether the personal guilt of company directors could ever be established or malefactors of great wealth put in jail.

Yet as he developed his Princeton reform programme, he gradually veered back to his earlier belief in the need for State action. As the opposition to his plans made him conscious of the power of money, so increasingly in his speeches he attacked first the exclusiveness which sought to perpetuate the Clubs, and then the money-dominated society that sought to dictate how the University should organise itself. Even among persons who would have little interest in Princeton as such his reputation as a politician rose, even though his actual political position seems not to have been clearly evaluated. For his positive proposals appear hardly to justify the enthusiasm with which he was coming to be regarded by the advocates of reform, while the Conservatives who regarded him as "safe" seem to have been blind to his advocacy of the need for leadership in American politics and to his assertions that government should be the servant of the whole people and not of any one particular interest only.

There can be little doubt that this sharpened appreciation of the power of money led him to pay more attention to the expansion of big business going on in the world outside and its destruction of the traditional Jeffersonian society of small men. Thus around 1910 Wilson began to move away from the idea that individual morality is an adequate instrument of reform and towards positive action on the part of government, which, because it is the servant of the whole people, should be neutral as between particular interests. Its object should be to guarantee free competition and to keep the channels of economic activity open to all.

101

Doubtless, too, he perceived that such a shift, aligning him as it did with contemporary Progressivism and the Liberal spirit of America, would help him to achieve the political ambitions which were already stirring within him. The curious thing is that the very Conservatives who proposed to nominate him as Democratic candidate for the Governorship of New Jersey did not see that he was swinging away from their party line and was coming to represent the views of Main Street rather than Wall Street. Wilson was, in fact, being urged to enter the political lists by a combination of the very elements which the Progressives were fighting, but the New Jersey Democratic party wanted office at all costs, and expected to be able to control him when elected, despite his assertions of independence. One would almost say that they did not take him seriously, and perhaps that is part of the explanation.

Chapter Five

New Jersey

AN American State and its government has no analogy in England, and least of all with any form of English local government, for its powers are original and sovereign. Indeed, the Constitution itself limits the powers of the Federal Government to those actually surrendered by the States. State governments are replicas of the Federal Government, and the position of the Governor who is elected by the State is similar to that of the President in that he is the Chief Executive, with wide powers of veto over State legislation, but is not a member of the Legislature, with which he can only communicate by Messages. The Governor of New Jersey holds office for three years at an annual salary (1910) of $10,000, the President of the United States for four years at an annual salary of $75,000.

New Jersey was, and, in fact, still is, a complex State containing diverse races, industries and social conditions. It is one of the transit States in which immigrants find temporary, and low-paid, work until they get used to the country and are ready to seek permanent homes elsewhere. On the coast are oystermen and fishers, inland market gardeners and dairymen, and in the towns merchants and industrial workers in a hundred trades, textiles predominating. It possesses two universities, Princeton and Rutgers, together with rural pockets of extreme illiteracy and small nineteenth-century villages where "the horse trader is more representative of the community culture than the automobile dealer." Its geographical situation between New York and Philadelphia made it a dormitory to the business men of those cities, who welcomed and supported the lax incorporation laws which assisted the formation of trusts.

In Wilson's time New Jersey was outstanding in the facilities it offered to industrial corporations; Steffens called it "The Mother of Trusts," a later writer "a green pasture for foaling corporations." They exercised the usual corrupt influence on the government, and their fees, in turn, lightened State taxes. Both political parties had strong machines which divided the spoils of government between them—a procedure which was justified by the argument that since, owing to the peculiar constitution of the State, it was normally difficult for the same party to elect both a Governor and a majority in the Legislature, some arrangement was necessary to avoid deadlocks over appointments and legislation. The Constitution further placed the Governor in a weak position, since he could not hold office for two consecutive terms and therefore had little chance of becoming a dominant factor in the government.

Wilson himself regarded New Jersey as "a sort of laboratory in which the best blood is prepared for other communities to thrive on," and added, "we have always been inconvenienced by New York on the one hand and Philadelphia on the other . . . the whole question of the regulation of corporations and the right attitude of all trades, their formation and conduct . . . centre in New Jersey more than in any other single State of the Union" (1911). It was, in fact, a seething mass of Liberal and reactionary forces, the former headed by George L. Record, a Progressive Republican, the latter comprising the orthodox party leaders on both sides, and notably ex-Senator James Smith, the Democratic boss. Thus although the fourth smallest State in size, it was no unworthy proving-ground for Wilson's political skill, the practicability of his political ideas and the genuineness of his ardour for reform. Moreover, the Governorship of a State is very like a smaller Presidency. "Training in the duties of the one fits for the duties of the other" (*Congressional Government*).

Smith used the full strength of the machine to force Wilson's nomination for Governor through the Democratic Party Convention of September 15th, 1910, in the face of the opposition of the Progressive elements in the party, whose hostility towards Smith and scepticism about Wilson were not allayed by Wilson's statement that he had given no pledges or promises as a condition of nomination. It was not until it heard his acceptance speech that the hitherto sullen Convention became enthusiastic in his support. Wilson campaigned for Governor on a reform programme embodying proposals for the prevention of electoral corruption, for economy and reorganisation of the State administration, control of corporations and equalisation of taxation. Particularly prominent and precise were his statements that he was opposed to the boss system, and if elected would act independently of it. He was elected by a plurality of 49,000 votes, and at the same time the Democrats secured a majority in the State Legislature.

This surprising result did not enlighten Smith as to the strength of the reforming wind now blowing through the States, and he promptly ran head-on into a contest with Wilson which provided a startling demonstration of the latter's powers.

Wilson had made it a condition of his acceptance of the nomination that Smith should not stand again for the United States Senate, and therefore in the Democratic primary a certain James E. Martine had been selected. Since at that time Senators were elected by the State Legislatures, the Democratic candidate was sure of election, and Smith therefore proclaimed his

intention of standing, confident that Wilson
would ignore this plain violation of his previous
undertaking. He little knew his man. When a
personal appeal failed, Wilson went into action.
He did not approach the State Legislature, but
denounced Smith in the Press and in public
meetings, where he dwelt not on the qualities of
Martine (which, except for a lifelong adherence
to Democratic principles, were few), but on the
right of the people to have their expressed
desires fulfilled, and not set aside by a political
boss. The force of public opinion thus aroused
proved greater than the presumed strength of
Smith's political machine, and the Legislature
duly elected Martine. Here was the first example
on a wider scale of the Wilson technique, foreshadowed at Princeton, of going over the heads
of representatives to the people themselves. Its
success could not but confirm Wilson in his
belief that, when the people had an issue clearly
and properly placed before them, they would
form a sound judgment, or, in other words,
would agree with him.

The short and successful struggle with Smith
made it clear that Wilson regarded himself as
leader of the Democratic party in the State. But
it was also in tune with his views on executive
leadership that he should also regard himself as
representing the whole electorate. Thus after
the election he equally consulted Republican
and Democratic reformers, such men as Joseph

Tumulty (who became his private secretary) and George L. Record. With their aid and that of William S. U'Ren of Oregon, who converted him to the principles of the initiative, referendum and recall he devised the legislative enactments necessary for the achievement of his programme.

One of the supports of the power of the party caucus was the fact that candidates for Federal, State and local offices were selected in a carefully packed Party Convention, and then presented in such a mass as to swamp the power of the average elector to discriminate and thus to deprive him of full freedom of choice. In one New York election the ballot sheet was eight feet long. Wilson aimed at knocking out this prop by having the candidates chosen by direct vote of the party. Thus one of his first Bills was the Geran Bill—so-called from the name of its actual sponsor in the Legislature—to provide for Direct Primary selection of candidates. In March 1911 his Republican and Democratic opponents—for the Democratic majority in the Legislature was still smarting under the defeat of Smith—called a conference under the chairmanship of James R. Nugent, acting head of the Democratic party organisation, to determine the party line on this and the other measures that they knew Wilson had in store—in other words, to concert plans to prevent him fulfilling the promises made during the election campaign. Wilson took the unprecedented step of declaring his wish to be present, and presented his ideas and argued his case in such a way that the conference, designed to defeat his programme, ended by heartily endorsing it. The defeat of Smith and Nugent was now complete, and Wilson's position as acknowledged leader of the one-time boss-ridden State of New Jersey became a national portent.

This was followed by the Corrupt Practices Bill on similar lines to that enacted in Great Britain, which together with the Geran Bill went a long way towards clearing up the New Jersey political atmosphere. An Employers' Liability Act imposed on employers the liability to pay compensation for industrial accidents in the absence of specific agreements to the contrary, a provision designed to avoid the possibility that unqualified liability would be declared unconstitutional. A Public Utilities Bill established a commission to regulate, in the interests of consumers as well as of the producers, all operations of water, gas and electricity suppliers and telephone and tramway companies. A Bill was also passed authorising the voluntary adoption by any city of the Commission form of government—that is to say, administration by a small commission elected for two to three years and with a salaried mayor in place of a municipal council elected on party lines. Bryce had pointed out that local government was the weakest spot in American political life, and this was, at this time, one of the most favoured remedies. By 1915 the system had been adopted in twenty-four cities of the State, and New Jersey was fourth among the States in respect of the number of cities so governed.

As at Princeton, the first enthusiasm of the State for its new and remarkable ruler carried reform forward in a flood, until opponents began to recover from their first shock and to rally their forces. Thus, in November 1911, the elections gave back the traditional Republican majority in the Legislature, and it was clear that when that body met in the following March, Wilson's power to carry out further reforms would be curtailed. And, in fact, throughout 1912 his attempts to reorganise the administration of the State Boards in the interests of economy and efficiency were largely blocked by the Legislature.

But again when failure or frustration seemed just round the corner, his path took a new turn and wider vistas opened before him. It appeared that Colonel Harvey's prognostication of half a dozen years before might come true. Indeed, the Colonel, in *Harper's Weekly*, was talking of Wilson as "predestined" to the Presidency. It is true that Wilson was no longer the Conservative he had considered himself to be in 1906, when his supporters were the "steady-going bankers," the men who feared W. J. Bryan, trade unions and the socialism of the West. At Princeton, and again in New Jersey, he had appealed over the heads of trustees, professors and politicians to the public and common people to democratise the University and the State. In 1907, in a brief prepared for Thomas Fortune Ryan, among others, he had praised trusts and combinations and turned away from positive use of the State as an instrument of reform. Now he was using the machinery of government to clear up politics, and was contemplating its use to protect the public from exploitation by trusts and combinations, and shareholders from the manipulating and watering of stock, by the so-called "Seven Sisters" Bill, which he pressed upon the New Jersey Legislature in his last official Message. Addresses up and down the country were marking him out as the candidate to accomplish Progressive reforms under the Democratic banner.

Wilson was not unwilling to undertake the office of President. Once when, in conversation, the question was raised whether anyone could really wish to be President, he is said to have replied, "I should. I know a whale of a lot about the Constitution of this country, and I'd rather like to watch the wheels go round." But to achieve this it was necessary to consolidate the Southern and Western Democratic votes. The former Wilson could claim by virtue of his birth, residence and upbringing. To obtain the latter he must secure the support of Bryan and jettison

Colonel Harvey and those earlier supporters of his Presidential aspirations who represented "that combination of boss politics, big business and journalism so hateful to the rising West." So Colonel Harvey was told, in December of 1911, that his support was embarrassing Wilson's claims to the Democratic nomination. The breach between the two men was skilfully represented by Wilson's friends as one with Wall Street also. Another Colonel took his place, "a Texas Warwick of mouselike timidity and almost Chinese self-effacement"—Edward M. House.

The first part of this description is less than fair, for House was an astute and experienced political tactician who had won his spurs fourteen years before. At this time his most valuable service was the assistance he gave in bringing together Wilson and W. J. Bryan. Though in his professorial days Wilson had not been unsympathetic to Bryan, yet when President of Princeton he had regarded him as a danger to the party and country, and in 1907 had expressed in a letter the hope that "we could do something, at once dignified and effective, to knock Mr. Bryan, once for all, into a cocked hat." In order to stir up discord between Wilson and Bryan, an old and bitter Princeton opponent published this letter in January 1912, only a few days before the traditional Jackson Day Dinner, at which the leaders of the Democratic party

meet for public discussion of the party pro-
gramme and, in a measure, to put Presidential
candidates through their paces. It failed, however, to disturb the concord which Colonel
House had achieved all over the South between
the friends of the Presbyterian elder of Lincoln,
Nebraska, and those of his co-religionist of
New Jersey, nor the personal understanding of
Wilson's present position, which Josephus
Daniels, a fighting pro-Wilson newspaper editor
of North Carolina, managed to implant in
Bryan's mind on his way to Washington. There
was no formal alliance, but Bryan was the
spokesman of the West and of the farmers,
representative of the older America that was
Protestant and Radical and homespun. Moreover, he controlled their votes, and his support
would not only be decisive in the Democratic
Convention to choose the Presidential candidate,
but equally in the election to follow.

For Wilson was not the only candidate for the
Democratic nomination. Others in the field were
Democratic nomination. Others in the field were
Bryan and Speaker of the House of Representatives; Governor Harmon, of Ohio, once member
of the second Cleveland Cabinet; and Oscar
Underwood, author of the proposed Democratic
tariff which was to take the place of the disastrous Payne-Aldrich tariff of President Taft.
Each had strong conventional claims to the party
nomination, and each had the support of the

party machine in various parts of the country. Each, however, represented the Conservative wing, Harmon's strength being in the North, Clark's in the Central States, where Thomas Fortune Ryan was an influential supporter, and Underwood in the lower South. It was understood that the three had agreed to pool their interests as against Wilson. In fact, only through the courage and management of Daniels and House did Wilson get any substantial party support in the broad region of the South, where he was the most popular candidate. The custom of the Democratic Convention required an affirmative vote of two-thirds of the delegates to secure nomination, and in the early days of 1912 Wilson had no assurance of more than half the six hundred votes that would be necessary. For Bryan and his friends lay low till its very opening.

In 1912 the Republican Convention met to choose their candidate early in June at Chicago. The result was disastrous to the party, for while the Republican National Committee used the power of the party machine to ensure Taft's acceptance by the Convention, Theodore Roosevelt was also nominated by a rival Convention as the head of a new Progressive movement. With the Republicans thus split, it was clear that the Democrats would win the Presidential election, just as it had been clear in 1860 that the Republicans would win it after a similar rupture of the old Democratic party. On that occasion the Republicans had nominated Lincoln. Whom would the Democrats nominate now? With victory in their grasp, it was clear that their Convention would be a stormy one, for while to the Conservative element it seemed a heaven-sent chance to regain office and break finally the influence of Bryanists and reformers, in fact the single condition of Democratic success was that they too should nominate a Progressive candidate on a Progressive platform.

The Democratic Convention met on June 25th at Baltimore. Clark held a majority of delegates pledged to vote for him, but Harmon and Underwood each held enough to prevent his nomination on the first ballot. Wilson's support was based on the Texas delegation, rounded up by House, on the two Carolinas won and held by Daniels, on Wisconsin, where Joseph E. Davies (later Ambassador to Moscow) had secured seventeen out of twenty-six delegates, and on New Jersey and Pennsylvania, which he had himself secured. The reactionary character of the Democratic National Committee and their intention to make Clark the nominee was shown by their appointment of Alton B. Parker, a Tammany Hall man and 1904 Presidential candidate, as temporary chairman instead of Bryan. But Parker's victory was narrow and even Pyrrhic, for popular reaction was immediate and critical, and Bryan's position was actually strengthened when the Convention elected as permanent Chairman a Progressive from Kentucky who was a friend of Bryan and always recognised him when he wished to speak. Political meteorologists noted that when Clark's name was proposed to the Convention, the applause lasted sixty-five minutes; Wilson's name received an ovation of seventy-five minutes; for comparative purposes we may note that Bryan in 1908 had been cheered for eighty-seven minutes.

The contest was clearly between Clark and Wilson, and Bryan, in a dramatic resolution, called on the delegates to renounce any candidate "who is the representative or under obligation to . . . Thomas F. Ryan . . . or any other member of the privilege-hunting and favour-seeking class." This startling presentation of the issue as between freedom and privilege produced pandemonium in the hall, ably abetted by the young State Senator from Albany, Franklin D. Roosevelt, who had come to Baltimore to try to persuade the Convention that New York State really wanted Wilson, despite the attitude of the official delegates, and managed by a trick to get a crowd of supporters into the hall—political airborne troops, as it were—who swamped the cries for Clark raised by the political regulars. The nomination of Clark was thenceforth hopeless, and when first Bryan, and then Sullivan, the Democratic boss of Illinois, publicly transferred their votes to Wilson, the latter's success was assured.

The platform on which the Democratic party decided to fight the election included most, if not all, of the causes for which reformers had been arguing since the turn of the century, or even earlier. Its economic plans included tariff revision, anti-trust legislation, a Federal income tax, rural credits and the conservation of natural resources; in the political sphere a Presidential primary and a single term of office for the elected President were proposed; in international affairs the independence of the Philippines and free passage through the Panama Canal for American coastwise shipping. In his acceptance speech Wilson substantially endorsed the platform, with special emphasis on its provision for financial reform, but it was clear that his conception of his position as leader of the party and of his function, if elected, as leader of the nation would forbid him to consider himself as necessarily bound by it. Thus more significant than the specific terms of the platform itself was the fact that although, in conformity with Jeffersonian tradition, it insisted that Federal legislation should be additional to and not a substitute for State legislation, this insistence was somewhat perfunctory and the main tenor of the platform called for a substantial exercise of Federal powers as the national situation might demand. This implied that the Democratic party was moving away from its old doctrine of the fundamental inviolability of State Rights, and in that case it was possible for an energetic President to convert it into an effective instrument of national reform. If Wilson were elected, it was certain that he would attempt such a conversion.

The orthodox Republicans supporting Taft stood on their candidate's record as President—a weak plank—and added to it proposals to prosecute trusts, for currency reform, conservation and a strong Navy, while Theodore Roosevelt's supporters borrowed impartially from both parties.

Thus the three chief candidates, and Debs, who was standing as the Socialist candidate, had very much the same programme. As for Wilson and Theodore Roosevelt, their programmes were almost indistinguishable, whether from one another or from those of Bryan's earlier candidatures if his silver proposals be omitted. Wilson and the Democrats had the clearer tariff proposals, while Roosevelt was more explicit on social and industrial reform, and each in some measure preached the doctrine of regulation. The main difference between them was not the direction of policy, but the probability of its execution. Seven years earlier, Sir William Harcourt had said of English parties, "We are all socialists now." Some similar phrase, using the term Progressives, might well have been used about the American election of 1912, were it not for the fact that in American Presidential elections striking differences of policy between the candidates is the exception rather than the rule.

Thus the country was not being called on to decide the direction of the policy it required—for that had already been made clear in the party conventions—but to decide how fast and how firmly it desired that policy to be pursued. The fight was therefore primarily between Theodore Roosevelt and Wilson. The former seemed the more advanced, and his campaign, which had much of the roaring enthusiasm and occasional irreverence of a revivalist meeting, attracted those voters who were disgusted with the regular party leaders, but through sectional bias or historical and family tradition could not bring themselves to vote with the solid South. Wilson, erstwhile professor and moderate Liberal, struck a more thoughtful, cautious and idealistic note in his speeches and surely did not show his full mind. Perhaps he did not yet know it himself, and certainly it was permissible to doubt, as many did, whether he would rise to the opportunity presented to the old party of Jefferson, Jackson and 1896.

It was due to these doubts that, although Wilson had a majority in the Electoral College, he only obtained a minority (42 per cent.) of the popular votes cast—less, in fact, than Bryan had received in any of his campaigns. The centre of his strength was in the old alliance of the South and West, assured to him by the support of Bryan. It was only in the States lying below the 36th parallel, and in Kentucky and Virginia, that he obtained clear majorities; Theodore Roosevelt carried Pennsylvania, Michigan, Minnesota, California, Washington and South Dakota, while Taft secured only Utah and Vermont. In the remaining States Theodore Roosevelt and Taft between them received a majority of votes. Thus Wilson was a minority President, as Lincoln had been, but the votes cast for the Progressive principles represented by himself, Theodore Roosevelt and Debs totalled 11 million out of a total of 15 million. Moreover, the Democrats secured majorities in both houses of Congress.

Wilson received the news of his election late in the evening of the election day, November 5th, and remarked quietly to his wife, as they retired to bed, that they would now be unable to carry out their plan for a visit to the Lake District. The news was repeated, with more excitement, next morning, when the coloured houseman plunged into his bedroom and exclaimed, "Guvnah, dey says as how you've done bin 'lected President."

He remained in office as Governor of New Jersey until three days before his Inauguration as President, on March 4th, 1913, partly to ensure that the "Seven Sisters" Bill passed the New Jersey Legislature, partly, so his enemies alleged, in order to draw the uttermost cent of his Governor's salary. The accusation was typical of the virulence of American politics and of the opposition which faced him.

assure that the 'Seven States' Bill passed the
New Jersey Legislature partly to his exertions
alleged. In order to duty the uttermost exent of
his Governor's salary. The occasion of... of
of the virulence of American politics and of the
opposition which faced him.

PART III

The United States, 1865—1913
(continued)

PART

The United States, 1865-1917

(Continued)

Chapter Six

Foreign Affairs 1865—1913

DURING the years between the Civil War and Wilson's election to the Presidency of the United States his country rose from comparative insignificance to the position of a World Power, in this, as in its internal development, passing in a single lifetime through stages which in other lands had required centuries. The events of these decades fall naturally into three periods: during the first, which lasted till 1872, Seward (1861–69) and Hamilton Fish (1869–77), as Secretaries of State, were clearing up unfinished business after the Civil War. Then follow twenty years of quiet, until about 1890, when the United States entered the second period—one of aggressive Nationalism, merging, not wholly imperceptibly, into one of Imperialism and world-politics. With these latter periods we associate Richard Olney, Secretary of State in Cleveland's second administration, and John Hay, who forms an interesting link with the older America, for he had been private secretary to Lincoln and Ambassador to London before being Secretary of State under McKinley and Theodore Roosevelt. In these two latter periods also we shall see developing the characteristic orientations of American foreign policy—on the one hand, towards the Pacific and the Far East; on the other hand towards the Caribbean and Latin America.

But we must first consider briefly two fundamental concepts of United States foreign policy —namely, the Monroe Doctrine, and what in later years was to be termed Isolationism.

The Monroe Doctrine of 1823 was essentially an assertion of the independence of the Western Hemisphere. Two events called it forth. The first was a claim advanced by Russia to territory south of Alaska as far as the 51st parallel; the other was the Congress of Verona, of 1822, in which the Powers of the Holy Alliance, having taken steps to crush democratic movements in Spain and Italy, discussed sending forces across the South Atlantic to compel some at least of the newly liberated nations of Latin America to return to their Spanish allegiance. This greatly alarmed Canning, the British Foreign Secretary, who suggested that Britain and America should take joint steps to block such intervention, a suggestion which Jefferson advised President Monroe to accept. Monroe, however, decided to take the advice of his Secretary of State, John Quincy Adams, that the United States should act independently, and in his Message to Congress in 1823 he included two declarations. The first was that the American continents "are henceforth not to be considered as subjects for future colonisation by any European Power." The second was that any European interposition "for the purpose of oppressing" the Latin-American States or "controlling in any manner their destiny" would be regarded as an unfriendly act. These two statements, behind whose "jaunty republican sound" an English note was perceptible, constituted the Monroe Doctrine; they sufficed to check the intentions of the Holy Alliance. One hundred and seventeen years later a similar threat called forth not Messages only, but the loan of arms, and Monroe's declaration made certain American participation in a European war for the second time in a generation.

At no time, however, has the United States bound herself to another nation by a Treaty of Alliance, and here we touch another fundamental, also enshrined in Presidential Messages —the Farewell Address of Washington and the First Inaugural of Jefferson. Washington, in 1796, warned his countrymen against cherishing "inveterate antipathies or passionate attachments" for other nations, and warned them particularly that Europe had interests that America did not share and was better left alone. Jefferson, in 1801, restated this view rather more firmly, advising that the country should seek honest friendship with all nations, but "entangling alliances with none"—a powerful and long-

127

remembered phrase. It is true that at the same time he recognised that if Napoleon Bonaparte were to re-establish French power in the Mississippi valley, "from that moment we must marry ourselves to the British fleet and nation." But this particular contingency never arose; indeed, eleven years later, the United States and Britain were at war over the actions of the same British fleet in insisting on the right of search. It was thus made easier for the United States to establish towards the outside world a traditional attitude always independent, sometimes positively aloof.

This attitude was not maintained consistently nor continuously, nor did it prevent American co-operation in international agreements of various kinds. For example, between 1865 and 1900 she signed more than a dozen agreements, covering such things as the laying of submarine cables, patent rights and the suppression of the African slave trade. In 1880 she joined a pact of European Powers to enforce the rights of foreigners in Morocco, and in 1862 adhered to the Geneva Red Cross Convention. Increasingly because of its vigorous growth, the United States became a force to be reckoned with in the affairs of other countries until in our own day, our two nations have become "considerably mixed up together."

The action of Confederate blockade runners based on the West Indies had naturally turned

the attention of the North to the Caribbean.
Seward therefore, as a safeguard against similar
action in the future, attempted to get a strategic
outpost by annexing Santo Domingo and buying
the Virgin Islands from Denmark for $7\frac{1}{2}$ million
dollars. The Senate, however, declined to ratify
his proposals. It was not until 1917 that the
islands were finally bought for 25 million
dollars, after the Danes had been informed that
the United States might find it necessary to take
possession of the islands if Denmark were
absorbed by a Great Power. The price paid was
a remarkable increase on that offered fifty years
earlier, but what would it have been twenty-
three years later?

Seward was more successful in his acquisition
of Alaska. Lest Britain should secure it, he
bought it from Russia for only $7\frac{1}{2}$ million
dollars. This was a long-term investment, because, apart from the gold rush of 1898, possession brought little immediate advantage to the
United States. Despite the railway built in 1914,
it was not until the Presidency of Franklin
Roosevelt that an intensive effort was made to
develop its natural and strategic resources.
Other long-term strategic moves by Seward were
to secure the right to drive a canal across
Nicaragua and to annexe Midway Island, west
of Hawaii, as a bastion to the latter.

With the withdrawal of the French from
Mexico and the purchase of Alaska, no Euro-

pean nations were left in the North American Continent. There still remained some unfinished business with England, notably the *Alabama* claims.

Relations with England, in fact, were undoubtedly strained. During the Civil War the masses of the English people had sympathised with the North, but the Government had hoped for a victory of the South, and Gladstone had even suggested a possible division of the country. Thus, though England was officially neutral, enforcement of neutrality had been lax and three Confederate ships, the *Alabama*, *Shenandoah* and *Florida*, had been allowed to leave port and equip themselves as commerce raiders. Seward claimed compensation both for the loss of ships and cargo directly due to their depredations and for the indirect loss due to increased cost of insurance and diminution of commerce. He made no headway while Lord John Russell was in office, but after the latter's retirement he negotiated the Clarendon Convention of 1869 for the adjudication of the claims. The Senate, however, rejected the Convention after a debate in which Senator Sumner charged Great Britain with responsibility for half the total cost of the war, some 2,125 million dollars. He further suggested that the cession of Canada would constitute an acceptable form of payment.

Such a suggestion was unlikely to improve

relations between the countries concerned, particularly since Canada herself had incurred expense between 1866 and 1870 in repelling attacks of Fenians based on United States territory. It was thus a remarkable tribute to the essential good sense on both sides that by 1871 Fish had succeeded in negotiating the Treaty of Washington, which provided that the *Alabama* claims should be arbitrated on the basis of three rules governing the duties of neutrals in time of war in respect of the use of ports and the fitting out of warlike vessels. Great Britain only reserved her view that the rules were not in force at the time the claims were made. The Treaty also included an expression of regret for the escape of the *Alabama* and other vessels from British ports and for their depredations, and provided also for the arbitration of certain fishery and boundary disputes. Fish had no desire to press the indirect claims, though American public opinion required that they be presented. The situation was smoothed over, however, by the proposal of C. F. Adams—the American member of the arbitration tribunal—to rule them out in advance. The tribunal in 1872 awarded the United States 15 million dollars on the direct claims, and found in favour of Great Britain on the fishery claims.

This remarkable vindication of the principle and practice of arbitration was the outstanding success of Grant's Presidency. He himself, with curious foresight, expressed his hope that some day there might be "some sort of Congress which will take cognisance of international questions of difficulty."

Between the *Alabama* settlement and about 1890 there is a quiet period in American foreign affairs. Various causes combined to bring it to an end. Of these, the most important was the increase in American manufactures, which demanded the outlet of external markets. After 1876 the balance of trade flowed increasingly in America's favour, and by 1900 the value of her exports was more than thrice what it had been thirty years earlier. Since this coincided with the "scramble" of the European Powers for Africa, it was not unnatural that America should turn her attention to the Far East, where the national spirit of adventure was already manifesting itself in widespread missionary activity, and to South America and the Caribbean. Just as other countries rationalised their Imperialism with such phrases as "the white man's burden," so America coined the phrase "manifest destiny" to justify this direction of her interests, and found in Captain Mahan the prophet of sea-power to justify her gradually growing island empire by the argument that a Navy needed island coaling stations, and islands needed naval protection. And while the Monroe Doctrine protected the Western Hemisphere from Europe, it did not protect it from the United States.

In fact, the United States early began to develop the Doctrine in a positive sense, with the object of improving both her political and commercial relations with other American countries. United States exports to South America had declined between 1860 and 1880, and in 1881 James G. Blaine, Secretary of State, called a Pan-American Conference to discuss a proposal for uniform tariffs, but he lost office on the accession of President Arthur and the invitations were cancelled. Eight years later, however, under President Harrison, he had another chance, and eighteen countries attended the Conference of 1889. Blaine's proposals were rejected as designed to increase U.S. influence, which they were, and the only outcome of the meeting was the establishment of the Bureau of American Republics (later called the Pan-American Union) as a clearing-house of commercial information. But Blaine continued his efforts, and the tariff of 1897 made provision for a series of reciprocity agreements, not only with Latin-America, but also with European countries. Despite the President's support, none of the treaties were ratified by the Senate. The moral was not lost on young Cordell Hull, whose Trade Agreements Act of June 1934 ushered in reciprocity agreements with some twenty-five countries made under Presidential authority only, nor on Woodrow Wilson, whose policy did much to allay the political uneasiness between North and South America, which persisted during these years and was in part the cause and in part the consequence of the failure to achieve economic harmony.

For if the United States was hesitant in establishing her economic position, she expressed her political pretensions in no uncertain terms. There had long been a dispute between Great Britain and Venezuela over the frontier line between the latter and British Guiana and in July 1895 Richard Olney, Secretary of State in Cleveland's second administration, sent a despatch to Lord Salisbury in which the British Premier was instructed in the relation of Washington's Farewell Address to the Monroe Doctrine and in the position of the United States in the Western Hemisphere. It concluded by asking whether Britain would accept arbitration.

The language of this Note was certainly arrogant, but it was also prophetic, and some sentences may usefully be quoted. Although torn from their context they may appear too extreme, nevertheless they express very clearly one aspect of the American attitude of mind which has long persisted:

The Monroe Administration therefore did not hesitate to accept and apply the logic of the Farewell Address by declaring in effect that American non-intervention in European affairs necessarily implied and meant Euro-

pean non-intervention in American affairs.
. . . It was therefore courageously declared
not merely that Europe ought not to interfere in American affairs, but that any European Power doing so would be regarded as
antagonising the interests and inviting the
opposition of the United States. . . . Today the
United States is practically sovereign on this
continent, and its fiat is law upon the subjects
to which it confines its interposition. Why?
It is not because of the pure friendship or
good will felt for it. It is not simply by reason
of its high character as a civilised State, nor
because wisdom and justice and equity are
the invariable characteristics of the dealings
of the United States. It is because, in addition
to all other grounds, its infinite resources
combined with its isolated position render
it master of the situation and practically
invulnerable as against any or all other
Powers.

All the advantages of this superiority are
at once imperilled if the principle be admitted
that European Powers may convert American
States into colonies or provinces of their
own. . . . If it were, the weaker countries
would unquestionably soon be absorbed, while
the ultimate result might be the partition of
all South America between the various European Powers. The disastrous consequences to
the United States of such a condition of
things are obvious. . . . We too must be armed
to the teeth; we too must convert the flower
of our male population into soldiers and
sailors, and by withdrawing them from the

135

various pursuits of peaceful industry, we too must practically annihilate a large share of the productive energy of the nation.

On December 17th, 1895, Cleveland sent a message to Congress reaffirming the American position and threatened to force Britain to accept his decision on the disputed boundary. Whether by accident or design, the move was shrewdly timed. On January 2nd, 1896, came the Jameson Raid and next day the Kaiser's telegram to Kruger. Great Britain was therefore in no mood to accept the challenge, and both Salisbury and Chamberlain made conciliatory statements in Parliament. Some secret diplomacy produced an agreement by Great Britain to arbitrate except in respect of territories held for fifty years, and as the result substantially upheld Britain's claim, her *de facto* position was secured. At the same time Cleveland and Olney equally gained their point, since Britain's final acceptance of the United States' interest in the issue went a long way towards admitting that the Monroe Doctrine was a part of the law of nations, despite Salisbury's earlier denial of this. But although the settlement was amicable, with apparent gains on both sides, the episode as a whole did not improve Anglo-American relations, but rather produced some suspicion of the high ideals set out in Olney's Note.

Provocative though the terms of the Note

were, the United States was more moved by apprehension of being drawn into an unwelcome war in the South American Continent than by jingoistic sentiments. Cleveland himself was no Imperialist, and his restraining influence and the financial panic of 1893 kept American ambition within bounds. But by the end of the decade Cleveland was gone and prosperity revived. The Spanish-American War and the invasion of Cuba were the natural consequences, though, as always, one must distinguish the ultimate from the immediate causes of the war.

Cuba is an island about the size of the State of Virginia, one-third of whose population was either black or of mixed race. After the Civil War there was a great inflow into Cuba of American capital, while at the same time recognition grew of its strategic position in the Gulf of Mexico and Caribbean Sea.

The chief industry in Cuba was the cultivation of sugar, and when the McKinley tariff placed it on the list of free imports, its output rose by 60 per cent. between 1889 and 1894. In the latter year, however, the Wilson-Gorman tariff took sugar off the free list and imposed a 20 per cent. import duty, producing in Cuba a catastrophic fall in prices and a severe depression. The result was an insurrection, of which the immediate cause was the poverty produced by the sudden change in American tariff policy, while the deeper cause was a popular demand for independence, based on an equal hatred of Spanish political oppression and of foreign economic exploitation.

Any people struggling to be free has, and rightly so, a claim on the sympathy of the United States. In this case sympathy was deepened by the fact that the struggle jeopardised 50 million dollars of American invested capital and an annual trade of 100 million dollars. The Americans, too, had a humanitarian dislike of the concentration camps with which Spain sought to subdue the insurgents, and the atrocities committed were publicised in particular by the *New York World* (owned by Pulitzer) and the *New York Journal* (owned by W. R. Hearst). In addition, Theodore Roosevelt, then Assistant Secretary of the Navy, "childish, rash and sanguinary," was pressing for a war to smarten up that Service. In 1897 Spain agreed to modify her policy of concentration camps and offered a degree of self-government to the Cubans. This concession came too late and the insurrection continued.

In 1898 two events further exacerbated anti-Spanish feeling. On February 9th the *New York Journal* published certain strictures passed on McKinley by the Spanish Ambassador in a private letter. Hard on the heels of this incident came, six days later, the sinking in Havana harbour of the battleship *Maine,* with the loss of over 200 lives. Popular feeling rose to fever heat, and on April 20th Congress declared war by a joint resolution.

Woodrow Wilson, in his *History of the American People*, characterised the Spanish-American War as a "war of impulse." It was very short, lasting only four months, and justified the gospel of Mahan and the aspirations of Theodore Roosevelt, because it was essentially won by the Navy. On May 1st Admiral Dewey destroyed the Spanish Pacific Fleet in Manila Bay in two sessions, with an interval for breakfast, this securing for the United States Spain's Pacific possessions. On July 3rd the loss of Cuba was made certain by the destruction of the Spanish Atlantic Fleet in Santiago Bay. On land, despite the dashing exploits of Roosevelt and his "Rough-riders," and picturesque reporting by such correspondents as Richard Harding Davis, the American Army made a deplorable showing, and only achieved victory because the Spaniards were even worse. Not only in Cuba, but also on the American mainland, the greatest inefficiency prevailed. War demands preparation and training, and the United States, not a bellicose nation, was trying to build up, and then move, under war conditions, a force of some quarter of a million men, mostly volunteers, with an organisation designed merely to cope with 25,000 regulars under peace conditions. Confusion and disorder were thus inevitable, but the U.S. War Department took its lessons to heart.

On August 12th Spain signed preliminaries of peace, and in the final Treaty, signed in Paris on December 10th, she relinquished all sovereignty over Cuba, ceded to the United States Puerto Rico and other West Indian islands, together with Guam in the Marianas, and handed over the Philippine Islands for 20 million dollars. This latter acquisition was fiercely opposed in Congress by both Democrats and Republicans as being unconstitutional and a violation of the American tradition of government by the consent of the governed, since the Filipinos, like the Cubans, had declared their independence. The Treaty was only ratified by a very narrow margin on February 6th, 1899.

Paradoxically enough, in view of later developments, the fight for ratification was led by Senator Henry Cabot Lodge, who argued that to reject the Treaty "would be a repudiation of the President and humiliation of the whole country in the eyes of the world, and would show we are unfit as a nation to enter into great questions of foreign policy." It is worth noting also that W. J. Bryan, although opposed to Imperialism, supported ratification on the ground that the terms of the Treaty represented the popular will and that Congress must follow the verdict of the people. Twenty years later Woodrow Wilson tried to mobilise both these points of view in favour of the Treaty which he negotiated.

After 1902 Cuba received her independence, subject to the provisions of the Platt Amendment, which gave the United States a veto on Cuba's relations with foreign Powers and a right of intervention. This right was exercised in 1906, when the island was occupied till 1909, and again in 1912, when Taft sent marines to protect United States interests. With the passage of time and the increased American economic penetration of the island, which for all practical purposes came to be controlled by the National City Bank of New York, the necessity for the political control represented by the Platt Amendment diminished in the minds of many Americans, who realised, moreover, that its existence was an obstacle to the full achievement of friendly relations with the Latin-American States. It was finally repealed in 1934.

The problem of the Philippines was more complex. Possession of the islands would provide a jumping-off ground for trade with China and a strategic outpost against Japan, while if the United States did not take the islands, it seemed certain that they would be acquired by Germany, already a dangerous trade rival. On the other hand, annexation was opposed by anti-Imperialists, Republican and Democratic alike, who argued that annexation "without the consent of the governed" was a violation of the

American ideal abroad, which would lead to further violations at home, and that occupation would entangle the United States in Eastern politics and involve just that typical increase in military and naval commitments deprecated in Richard Olney's Note. Provision for the acquisition of the islands was written into the Treaty of Paris, but the McEnery Resolution, attached to the Treaty, was widely held to imply that the independence and self-government of the islands was America's ultimate aim. In the last analysis, however, the strength of the sentiment for Philippine independence depended on the extent to which the sugar and tobacco States would suffer from the free importation of island-grown produce.

The Spanish-American War was a typical expression of the forces of Nationalism and Imperialism which were driving European countries also to war at the end of the nineteenth century. It marks a turning-point in American history because it crowned the national growth of the previous thirty years, as did the Franco-Prussian War for Germany, and in each case an acquisition of territory set the seal on the national unity produced by the common effort. Not only did the inhabitants of different parts of the country get to know one another— though the drafts were less mixed than in the later World War—but particularly the participation of ex-Confederate officers on an equality with Northerners healed Southern pride, and the divisions of the Civil War may be said to have been erased at St. Juan Heights.

Moreover, it improved Anglo-American relations, since Great Britain had looked with a friendly eye on the country's exploits, while other European Powers had been unfriendly and, in the case of Germany, actually obstructive. The effect on the South American States, however, was less happy, for to them the war, although against the ancient enemy, appeared as an act of aggression and an uncertain augury for the future. The United States felt itself now at last a World Power, and began to cultivate a limited sphere of external interests in the Pacific and Caribbean and a positive attitude to China.

Chinese ports had been open to United States trade by the Treaty of Hwangshia in 1844, but by the end of the century it seemed clear, not only to the American missionaries who wanted to convert the Chinese, but also to the industrialists and traders who wanted to sell textiles and oil, that America was in danger of being frozen out, and in that case the advantages of holding the Philippines would be neutralised. In 1899 John Hay addressed a circular to the Powers suggesting that they pursue a policy of equality of tariffs, harbour dues and railway rates, which later became known as the "Open Door." Great Britain formally agreed to Hay's proposal, but all the other Powers, except Russia, merely expressed approval. Russia returned a definite rejection. Hay, however, expressed himself satisfied and announced that the agreement of all the Powers was "final and definite." Since this was not the case, the effect was not so much to bind the other Powers to any agreed course of action as to commit the United States to an interest in Eastern affairs. Hence, when the Boxer Revolution broke out in 1900, the United States could not avoid taking part in the expedition to Pekin and a share in the Chinese indemnity, although more than half of this she ultimately returned to China.

Hay did succeed in preserving China from the dismemberment which might have followed that expedition, but with the passage of time it became clear that the United States was not prepared indefinitely to redeem the implied commitment to maintain Chinese integrity. Neither Bryan's protest in 1915 nor that of Henry Stimson in 1932 did anything to check the progress of Japan in Manchuria. But at the time Hay's statement did do something to delay the partition of China, gave prestige to the United States and, in so far as it helped British commercial interests in the East, disposed Britain in favour of American policy in the Caribbean and so kept Anglo-American relations in good trim.

The foreign policy of Theodore Roosevelt

recognised that the United States was now a
World Power, but, with one exception, he was
not aggressive. The exception is, of course,
Panama.

The idea of a canal joining the Atlantic and
Pacific had long been in the minds of Americans,
but, to the fury of Theodore Roosevelt, the
Colombian government hesitated to ratify the
agreement to cede the necessary strip of territory. To overcome this hitch both the President
and State Department connived at a revolt in
the City of Panama, which on November 3rd,
1903, was duly carried out by the City Fire
Brigade, protected by the United States cruiser
Nashville which, by a curious coincidence, had
arrived the previous day. On November 18th
the new Republic gave the United States a
perpetual grant of the Canal Zone, the right to
fortify it if necessary, and the right to maintain
order in the cities of Panama and Colon.

Before construction could begin in earnest,
the sanitary work of Reed in Cuba had to be
duplicated in Panama, but by 1906 Colonels
Gorgas and Goethals had freed the Zone from
yellow fever and malaria. The Canal was declared open for commercial traffic in August
1914 with a parade, to which the State Department invited all Navies, including that of
Switzerland. It was finally completed in 1920.

Roosevelt prided himself on having gone
ahead and secured the Canal while Congress and

the purists were discussing fine points of constitutional law. But his methods did not help friendly relations with Latin-America, which saw with alarm and hostility such unmistakably imperialistic treatment of a small and helpless neighbour. On the wider stage of world politics, Theodore Roosevelt played the diplomatic game with the crowned heads of Europe in something of the jaunty manner of Palmerston. Although professing dislike for power diplomacy, he actually practised it with some skill. His personal share in ending the Russo-Japanese War and initiative in calling the Algeciras Conference raised the power and prestige of his country and further established its right to be consulted on world affairs. Unfortunately the country as a whole did not want any such right, and it is significant that Taft made no move during the second Morocco crisis of 1911.

The truth was that both in domestic and foreign affairs Roosevelt's policy was intensely personal, and it was his personality rather than his policy which aroused such enthusiasm among the nation at large. He did indeed have a glimpse of that wider vision of the "one world" and of America as an active and responsible member of it, to which a later and more meteoric Republican, Wendell Willkie, also tried to open the unwilling eyes of his party. In negotiating the Treaty of Portsmouth,

Roosevelt risked a moral commitment of the American people to membership of the Anglo-Japanese alliance, which was contrary to their basic principle of non-involvement in the affairs of other nations. It was fortunate that its fulfilment was not demanded. For at that time even fewer Americans than in the nineteen-forties thought that matters in Europe or the Far East could concern them.

Roosevelt's failure to produce loyalty to his principles as well as to himself is the measure of his failure as a leader. It was to be Wilson's also, and more tragically because Wilson's theories were both more comprehensive and more coherent than Roosevelt's. For while in home affairs and in so far as he attempted to convert into a reality the popular ideals of democracy and liberty Roosevelt was a Progressive, in foreign affairs he was frankly Nationalistic. The Progressive movement was not strong enough to make him apply abroad the principles by which they set such store at home, notably that of democratic self-determination. It was left for Wilson to try to bring these two sides into harmony or, if you will, to extend the theory and practice of American Liberalism to include both home and foreign relations.

By contrast with that of Roosevelt, the foreign policy of Taft was a succession of failures, which it is kinder to pass over swiftly. In defence of Taft, it may be argued that they were due less to his own gentle nature than to the unco-operative behaviour of the Senate, which rejected arbitration treaties concluded with Great Britain and France in 1911 and treaties with Nicaragua and Honduras similar to those successfully negotiated by Roosevelt with Santo Domingo. In China, in 1909, he attempted to meet Japanese penetration by an international loan, but the proposal was declined, perhaps not unnaturally, by Russia and Japan. He then proposed that United States bankers should participate in a four-Power loan to finance railway construction, but both this and his Central American policy were dubbed "Dollar Diplomacy" and were repudiated by Wilson. The failure of the Canadian Reciprocity Treaty has already been mentioned.

There remains to note the so-called "Lodge Corollary" to the Monroe Doctrine. This was a Resolution introduced by Senator Lodge and passed by the Senate on August 2nd, 1912, to the effect that the United States "could not see without grave concern" the occupation by any non-American Power of any potential military or naval base in the American Continent. Monroe would surely have approved the Resolution, and it followed strictly the lines laid down by Richard Olney and Theodore Roosevelt. Its immediate object was to stop the proposed purchase of Magdalena Bay in South California by a Japanese fishing company, though at the cost of further aggravation of Latin-American opinion, which viewed it as merely another attempt by the United States to tighten her control of the Western Hemisphere. But the Resolution also made it inevitable that after the fall of France in 1940 the United States should sooner or later declare war on Germany, either to preserve from annexation the French and Dutch colonies in the Caribbean or to prevent German penetration in Latin-America. It is an irony of history that it should have been moved by the most vigorous and successful opponent of Wilson and of American participation in the League of Nations.

no further disposition on the part of the American
Republic, it was desired to be merely another
attempt by the United States to extend its control of the Western Hemisphere. But the reason
put also indicated, more than that after the fall of
France all republicks in either sense should work
its safe designs upon Germany, either to prevent a republican simulation of French, and Dutch
colonies in the Caribbean or to prevent German
possession in Latin America. It is an issue of
politicks that it should have been agreed to the
public figures and universal opposition of British
of American aspiration of the League of
Nations.

PART IV

Woodrow Wilson, Twenty-eighth President of the United States

Chapter Seven

The New Freedom at Home

THE American Presidency has often been compared with the British Premiership, to the latter's disadvantage. It is true that the President appears to combine the positions of King and Premier, but his powers are largely illusory, and because of the constitutional separation of the Executive and Legislature, he lacks the resources open to a Prime Minister under a system of Parliamentary government. If Congress passes legislation of which the President disapproves, he may indeed veto it, but he cannot force a reversal of a decision of Congress by threatening to dissolve it and appeal to the country, for the times of Congressional elections are fixed by the Constitution, and nothing, not even a state of war, can vary them. Similarly, Congress cannot send the President to the country by an adverse vote, for the times of Presidential elections are similarly predetermined. Wilson did on one occasion contemplate a referendum on his continuance in office, but he never carried it out.

Wilson was very well aware of the limitations on the President's power. He had written, "The

Presidency is very far from being equal to a first-rate Premiership," for "a Premier must keep himself in favour with the majority, a President need only keep alive." Theodore Roosevelt, in the course of his campaign, had accepted a suggestion of McCarthy of Wisconsin that the principle of popular recall should apply to the President, but he had never made his view public, fearing to be accused of wishing to press the obvious corollary—namely a Presidential term that should be otherwise unlimited. By contrast, the Democratic programme advocated a single term only for Presidents—a plank it owed to W. J. Bryan. Wilson, however, did not accept this, on the ground that if the people had so desired, they would have said so earlier; personally, he did not favour a limit to the number of Presidential terms, and would have taken a third term himself had it proved possible. Meanwhile, he was prepared to explore to the limit the powers which under the Constitution the President by wise leadership might be able to exercise, for "the President is at liberty . . . to be as big a man as he can" (*Constitutional Government in the United States*).

He was inaugurated on March 4th, 1913, accompanied to the Capitol by the retiring President as is customary. It would not have been extravagant to deduce something of the future from the appearance of the two men, for even physically they were a notable contrast. Some chance incident amused the two of them as they stood together on the Capitol terrace, and the moment was captured by a Press photographer, who has shown Taft enjoying the "habitual easy laughter of a fat man," while Wilson's merriment was rather the momentary relaxation of a hard-trained athlete.

The essence of Wilson's policy had been fittingly expressed by his speech at the Jackson Day Dinner fifteen months earlier. "The matter has been that the government of the country was privately controlled and that the business of this country was privately controlled; that we did not have genuine representative government and that the people of this country did not have control of their own affairs. What do we stand for to-night, and what shall we stand for as long as we live? We stand for setting the government free and the business of the country free." His campaign addresses had elaborated this theme, and the title of the volume into which they were collected by W. B. Hale gave to his programme the name of the "New Freedom." Essentially its aim was the restoration of freedom to the people by the abolition of the private control of economic power. A truly democratic system should give equal opportunity for development to all, and this would be achieved by establishing genuinely free competition, in which the little man would survive and could advance.

Thus all consolidation of power, and especially of money power, should be opposed, because it led to countermoves to consolidate the power of labour and thus to social conflict and even to Socialism. These general principles Wilson applied to the specific issues of the time.

His Inaugural Address, launching his policy of the New Freedom, was one of the shortest, if not the shortest, ever made, a bare fifteen hundred words. After an analysis of American progress and its physical and spiritual cost—"we were very heedless and in a hurry to be great"— he "itemised with some degree of particularity the things that ought to be altered"—a stultifying and ill-conceived tariff, a restrictive system of banking and currency, an industrial system which exploits without renewing the natural resources of the country, neglected agriculture and a disregard of the public health. The indictment was drawn, not in such picturesque terms as W. J. Bryan had used in 1896, but none the less with equal force and with the precision of the scholar and political scientist. There could be no mistake about his intentions, and, further, he declared that what he proposed "will be no cool progress of mere science," but a high moral endeavour. It was a moral contest between good and evil upon which the nation had now entered.

"This is not a day of triumph; it is a day of dedication. Here muster, not the forces of party, but the forces of humanity."

Chief Justice White, an ex-Confederate soldier and Roman Catholic, administered the oath of office to the new President—a Southern-born Presbyterian from a Northern State. As if to emphasise the seriousness of his intentions, Wilson dispensed with the usual Inaugural Ball, to the intense disgust of Washington society and tradesmen.

For carrying out his plans Wilson had a Democratic majority in each House of the sixty-third Congress of the United States. The fifty-third Congress—the first of Cleveland's second term—had had a similar complexion, and this, as we have seen, had prompted Wilson to urge Cleveland to lead the nation. Wilson himself was now in a like position. But the fifty-fourth Congress had had a Republican majority in both Houses, and Wilson, therefore, was determined to work fast. In fact, the programme outlined in his Inaugural Address was substantially completed in nineteen months.

His Cabinet was already chosen, an able team if not brilliant. The members of an American Cabinet stand in a more personal relation to the President than do British Ministers even to the Prime Minister, being in fact what the latter are only in theory—namely, Secretaries to the Chief Executive for various purposes, finance, foreign affairs, etc. Thus they do not sit in Congress and, being responsible only to the President, and not to Congress, are seldom drawn from that body; it is, in fact, the exception rather than the rule for any member of an American Cabinet to have had previous Congressional experience.

Moreover, in choosing his Cabinet the President must bear in mind the need to maintain party support and local loyalties by a fair distribution of offices among the various sections of the party and country. This is especially the case with a Democratic President, if only because there have been so few of them since the Civil War, so that the opportunities to reward loyal party members have been similarly infrequent. In 1913 the need to unite the party after the violent contest over the Presidential nomination was particularly compelling. Thus Wilson's distribution of offices illustrated the geographical basis of the party victory, for of the nine Cabinet members, four were from the South and two from the West; none were from New England, although Wilson had had the support of Massachusetts.

The Secretaryship of State went to W. J. Bryan, as was inevitable, not only as a reward for his efforts at Baltimore, but to ensure the support of Western Radicals and as a pledge that there would be no sell-out to Wall Street. That he was a well-known pacifist encouraged some foreign countries to suppose that United States foreign policy would be correspondingly ineffective. McAdoo, a lawyer who had organised the construction of the Hudson Tunnels and had been Wilson's 1912 campaign manager, was appointed Secretary of the Treasury. The appointment as Secretary of the Navy of Josephus Daniels had at first a depressing effect, for he was a pacifist like Bryan and, moreover, a teetotaller with an avowed ambition, which he subsequently realised, to make the American Navy "dry." But he proved a strong Secretary in other ways, and with Franklin D. Roosevelt as Assistant Secretary cleared up the mess caused by ten years' stagnation under big business and political jobbery. (Roosevelt had refused the post of Collector in the New York Custom House, although Chester Arthur had found it a stepping-stone to the White House. He remained with the Navy Department for almost seven and a half years, until nominated as Vice-Presidential candidate in 1920.)

These, and others, might be regarded as amateur appointments, but for Postmaster-General Wilson chose a professional politician, A. S. Burleson, of Texas. The Postmaster-General has an importance denied to his British counterpart, in that he acts as the patronage secretary to the administration, a function founded on the fact that he has some 56,000 postmasterships to dispense to deserving party members of the lesser sort. These minor appointments also Wilson at first wished to keep in his own hands and to award on the basis of merit only; Burleson convinced him that this was utterly impossible and, moreover, that judicious allocation of these jobs would sweeten his relations with Congress. This was a valuable service in showing Wilson that he must consult with "the men on the Hill" as well as lead them. Indeed, to assist the President to pass measures through Congress and generally to attend to the political problems of government were among the chief functions of Bryan, Daniels and Burleson, while McAdoo and the others were chosen chiefly for their administrative ability.

Colonel House appointed himself a sort of one-man Cabinet Secretariat, button-holing Cabinet Members and persuading them to let him sort out their problems and present them in due priority to the President. This was as near as House permitted himself to come to the personal realisation of a novel he had published anonymously in 1912, just after the Presidential election, entitled *Philip Dru: Administrator,* in which the hero took over the government of the United States. Many of Philip Dru's policies, however, were carried out by Woodrow Wilson.

Wilson also tried to establish a press conference twice weekly, but the experiment was not wholly successful. He fundamentally distrusted the press, believing that reporters were constitutionally incapable of accurate reporting and were more interested in personalities than in principles or policy. Hence he gave them very little information and they received the impression, which was by no means erroneous, that he regarded these conferences as rather a battle of wits. This was doubly unfortunate, because—as we now see, though Wilson did not—the President's Press Conference is in many ways the American equivalent of Question Time in the House of Commons. Moreover, had Wilson been able to become and remain on friendly terms with the nation's press, it would have given him invaluable service in his later political campaigns. To so accomplished an orator the radio might well have proved a godsend.

In April Congress met in special session to hear Wilson's first Message outlining his legislative programme. He decided to deliver it in person, the first President to do so for over a century, and although it was referred to by some as a "speech from the throne," in general the action was applauded as an imaginative gesture symbolising the close association of the President with Congress and his position as also a part of the law-making machinery of the country.

The first item of business was the revision of the tariff. In his address to the roving Tariff

Commission at Atlanta in 1882 Wilson had said:

> "I maintain that manufacturers are made better manufacturers whenever they are thrown upon their own resources and left to the natural competition of trade,"

but the Democratic party was not, and never had been, a Free Trade party, and Wilson was forty years older now. Underwood of Alabama, Kitchen of North Carolina and Cordell Hull of Tennessee (who had entered Congress in 1906) had prepared a Bill revising the tariff, and this was accepted by Wilson and passed by the House of Representatives after a brief debate.

But it was well known that the real fight on the Bill would take place in the Senate, for although the Bill was not an out-and-out Free Trade measure, it did place on the free list a number of articles, such as wool, iron ore, steel rails, rough lumber and agricultural products, while sugar duties were to be reduced by one-quarter and abolished as from May 1916. Thus it was natural that Senators, for example, from Colorado and Louisiana, representing sugar interests, Western Senators from wool-producing States and the Southern citrus-fruit growers should be among the many who opposed the reductions accepted by the House of Representatives, where the more populous Northern States

162

had a preponderant voting strength. The lobby-ists therefore concentrated their attention on the Senate, using the established techniques of flooding individual Senators with letters and telegrams.

The Bill went to the Senate on May 8th, and the next day Wilson joined the Senate Finance Committee in conference upon it, the first President since Lincoln to confer with a Congressional committee. But when its slow progress appeared to challenge the effectiveness of his leadership, Wilson's reactions ran true to his earlier strategy. On May 26th he appealed to the people in a press statement attacking the lobby as composed of astute men who "seek to create an artificial opinion and overcome the interests of the public for their private profit." This produced a further flood of correspondence, this time in favour of the Bill, and provoked some resentment in the Senate, which felt that Wilson was not quite playing the game. But the effect was to hold the Democrats and insurgent Republican supporters in line and by focusing national attention on Washington to compel obedience to the President's will. It was the precursor of President Franklin Roosevelt's technique of the radio "fireside chat." As a result the Democratic caucus lined up behind the Bill, and on July 11th it was introduced on to the floor of the Senate. During the heat of summer Wilson kept Congress in Washington, participating himself in conferences with the Senate Committee, until the Bill was finally passed in September and received his signature on October 3rd.

It was his first triumph. Apart from the free list already referred to, the Act reduced the duties on over nine hundred articles, and the average level of duty was brought down from 42 to 27 per cent. Even if this was not Free Trade, and Wilson's claim to have freed the country from the conditions that bred monopoly was exaggerated, it was at least a notable defeat for the tariff policy that had ruled substantially unchallenged since the Civil War. Moreover, it worked smoothly, and during the ensuing year brought in more revenue than was expected. What its ultimate effect would have been we shall never know, for the War of 1914 radically altered the international economic position of the United States. The effect of Cordell Hull's Reciprocal Trade Treaties was to be similarly interrupted a generation later.

The ratification of the Sixteenth Amendment in February 1913 made it possible to offset by a Federal income tax the loss of revenue involved in the Underwood Tariff. These proposals were particularly the work of Cordell Hull, who had never approved the action of the Supreme Court in invalidating the income-tax provisions of 1893, which had been written by another Tennesseean, Senator Benton McMillan. The tax was regarded purely as a revenue measure, designed to bring in about 70 million dollars at the rate of 1–6 per cent. on incomes of 3,000 dollars or over, but it was recognised that its initial limited scope (for the application of existing British rates would have yielded 400 million dollars) left room for expansion. Thus in the war years 1914–19 it yielded 15,000 million dollars. In no sense was the tax regarded as an instrument of social reform. Nevertheless, it also provided a considerable body of information about the distribution of income in the United States, which provided ammunition for social reformers as well as basic facts for law-makers.

In 1916 the Underwood Tariff was supplemented by the setting up of a permanent Tariff Commission. This was an attempt to "take the tariff out of politics" and base it on a scientific appraisal of the facts and needs of the situation as shown by a careful investigation of all the aspects—economic, fiscal and administrative—of tariff laws. The first chairman was Professor Frank W. Taussig of Harvard. That Wilson should have decided to approach the problem in a spirit of research might not be surprising when we reflect on his scholastic past, although in that past he had vigorously opposed the creation of any such body. But 1916 was an election year, and it cannot have escaped his notice that Presidents who meddled with the tariff were not generally re-elected. In such circumstances to take the tariff out of politics was perhaps expedient.

Wilson did not wait for the passing of the Tariff Bill before starting Congress off on the second lap of its legislative course. On June 23rd, at the height alike of the Washington summer and the tariff struggle, he again appeared in person and presented his proposals for dealing with the banking and currency situation already outlined in his Inaugural Address.

The trouble went back to the time after the Civil War when the older State banking system broke down and Congress adopted the "National" system, whereby certain local banks obtained the right of note issue up to 90 per cent. of the face value of government bonds held by them. Backed thus, the currency was eminently "sound," but in its effect the system was deflationary in tendency, since if the market value of the bonds rose above their face value, the banks naturally tended to sell, while if it fell below, the government redeemed them. Either course led to a reduction of the currency. This was one of the reasons for the falling prices which, as we have seen, particularly enraged the farmers. Credit was restricted because the bankers could not or did not issue notes freely when needed, even at high interest rates, so that in order to obtain liquid resources would-be borrowers had to sacrifice securities, which the banks held until prices rose, when they resold profitably.

In the process money power was concentrated in a few banks in New York, who were able to cut off loans and so produce "financial crises" at will and, moreover, used their power with none of the sense of responsibility that a Central Bank organised by Federal statute might have imposed upon them. It was generally agreed that the "panic" of 1907 was a purely financial one due to currency shortage and the inelasticity of credit. As a result the Aldrich-Vreeland Bill had proposed the issue of currency against State and municipal securities and commercial paper, and the National Monetary Commission, instructed to report on the whole problem, had noted the concentration of money power in New York banks, an observation reinforced by the revelations of the Pujo Committee referred to in Chapter II.

But though there was agreement both on the nature of the malady and the principle of the cure, there was acute controversy over how the cure was to be compounded and administered. Conservative and banking circles favoured a central bank owned by private banking institutions and controlled by them. This was the essence of the proposals put forward by Senator Aldrich and endorsed by the American Banking Association. At the opposite pole of opinion the politically influential W. J. Bryan wanted the issue of notes to be a government function and the banking system to be under government control.

Wilson was no believer in a central bank, which was, in fact, ruled out by the 1912 Democratic platform, and himself favoured a system of regional reserve banks supervised by a central board at Washington. A Bill in this sense had been prepared by Carter Glass of Virginia (then Representative; Secretary of the Treasury 1918–20 and later Senator) and was presented to Congress on June 26th. That the Bryan group at first thought it too favourable to the bankers, while the bankers opposed it as too restrictive of their activities, is some evidence of its balance, although McAdoo feared that in seeking too nice a balance it might fall before the opposition of both Conservatives and Radicals. But when Wilson announced his opposition to banker representation on the board and that he favoured Federal Reserve notes being "obligations of the United States," Bryan announced his support, and in August the Bill was adopted as a Democratic Party measure. On September 18th it passed the House of Representatives by the substantial majority of 287 to 85.

In the Senate, however, debate was prolonged, as the bankers kept up their opposition. They were not, however, wholly united, for some of the most important Westerners saw a chance to shake the financial primacy of New York. Meanwhile the November elections went in Wilson's favour, and as time marched on even the New York bankers began to feel that any law would be better than continued uncertainty. Moreover, Wilson was refusing to let Congress adjourn for Christmas until the Bill was voted on. At last, on December 19th, the Federal Reserve Act passed the Senate by 54–34 and was signed by the President on December 23rd, unchanged in any point of principle from the form in which it had originally been introduced.

The Act divided the country into twelve Federal Reserve Districts, each with a Federal Reserve Bank, formed from the National Banks in the District. Private persons could not own stock in Federal Reserve Banks; they dealt with banks only. In them reserve funds were deposited, and from them member banks could borrow. The rate of interest was controlled by a central Federal Reserve Board consisting of the Secretary of the Treasury, the Comptroller of the Currency and five members nominated by the President and approved by the Senate. The inter-relation of local banks with the regional Federal Reserve Banks and of these with one another, and with the Board at Washington, made it possible to use all the resources of the system, if necessary, to enable member banks to maintain payments.

An elastic currency and credit system was thus

secured, but whether the further accumulation of money power in any centre or in the hands of any single financial group would be effectively prevented remained to be seen. The bankers at least could be well satisfied with the Bill as a whole, and might well feel that though they had lost the battle over the control of the issue of currency, they had not lost the whole campaign, for the men whom Wilson appointed to the Board were always conservative and frequently drawn from their ranks. The greater elasticity and wider distribution of banking facilities which the Act provided added immeasurably to the financial stability of the country, and not least in the years of war that followed.

One object of the Federal Reserve Act, however, was not at once fulfilled—namely, the provision of short-term credit for farmers at sufficiently low rates of interest. These needs of farmers had been mentioned in Wilson's message proposing the Bill, but its provisions did little to produce the desired result. Wilson had not been much interested in agriculture, until his Presidential candidature, when he was largely influenced by Walter H. Page, who suggested as Secretary of Agriculture David F. Houston (ex-President of the University of Texas and in 1912 Chancellor of the Washington University of St. Louis), one of the ablest members of Wilson's Cabinet, who became Secretary of the Treasury for a brief period in

1920. Not until 1916 were two measures passed which gave some reduction in farm interest rates and created better credit facilities for farmers. The Federal Farm Loan Act created a Federal Farm Loan Board and twelve regional Farm Loan Banks—much like the Federal Reserve System—deriving funds from member farm loan associations. They were authorised to make loans up to 70 per cent. of the value of farm lands and buildings for from five to forty years at rates not exceeding 6 per cent. A large number of such associations was formed, so that by the time of the Great Depression the Farm Loan Banks held over 1,000 million dollars of farm mortgages. The Warehouse Act of 1916 authorised licensed warehouses to issue against farm products receipts which farmers could use as negotiable paper. The Populists had proposed such a scheme a generation earlier.

The programme of the Inaugural Address was thus being shown to be no empty form of words, and from the Tariff and Currency Wilson turned to Trusts. These were more numerous and powerful in 1913 than in 1900, but when, in January 1914—just after the signature of the Federal Reserve Act—the great J. P. Morgan resigned from thirty out of his sixty-three directorships, this was hailed as a victory for Wilson and for public opinion, and Colonel House reported that it was largely taken to indicate that big business was prepared to go quietly. Wilson responded to this assumption in his Message to Congress about a fortnight later, in which he announced his belief that the antagonism between business and government was over and that they were now met together in a common endeavour to align business methods with public opinion and with the law.

Wilson did not object to bigness in business as such, but only when achieved by unrighteous means which crush the small business. His attack was therefore on monopoly rather than on size; business may well grow through competitive efficiency, but a Trust is an arrangement to get rid of competition and the efficiency that goes with it. His Message therefore contained five main recommendations: the prohibition of interlocking directorates; increased power to the Inter-State Commerce Commission to supervise railroads; a clarification of the existing anti-trust legislation; the punishment of individuals, not businesses, for violation of the law; and a Federal Trade Commission to guide business. These followed closely the measures long advocated by Louis D. Brandeis, whose views had influenced Wilson. But Brandeis regarded bigness as an evil in itself, while Wilson thought that it showed fitness to survive. Congress responded with the Clayton Anti-Trust Act, the Federal Trade Commission Act and the Rayburn Securities Act.

The first of these, signed on October 15th,

1914, forbade price discrimination, conditional sales, the acquisition of stock in competing businesses and interlocking directorates when the object of these manœuvres was to lessen competition or to create monopoly. The Inter-State Commerce Commission was given increased power over railroad finances. The officers of corporations were personally responsible for violations of the Act.

The Act also dealt with the position of labour unions, which had been regarded as Trusts or combinations in restraint of trade and subject to the provisions of the Sherman Act. Gompers had succeeded in tacking on to an Appropriations Bill (or Finance Bill) a rider designed to prevent unions from being prosecuted as Trusts but Taft had vetoed this on his last day in office. The Bill was subsequently passed again by Congress and Wilson signed it. In the Clayton Act, however, he went farther and specifically exempted unions from the provisions of the anti-trust laws and at the same time forbade the use of injunctions in labour disputes "unless necessary to prevent irreparable damage to property." Even then the extent of the "restraining order or injunction" that might be granted was severely circumscribed. The spirit of these provisions was set out in the opening statement "that the labor of a human being is not a commodity or article of commerce"—words which find an echo in Article 427 of the Treaty of Versailles and were themselves reminiscent of *Philip Dru*.

But the letter of the Act did not fulfil its object of giving labour a right of combination similar to that provided in Great Britain by the Trade Disputes Act of 1906. It was found that judges readily accepted pleas of "irreparable damage to property" and in granting injunctions were little hampered by the restrictions laid down. The "yellow-dog contract," whereby employers, as a condition of employment, bound workmen not to join unions, was not outlawed by the Act, nor were unions exempted from corporate responsibility for torts committed by their members.

Nor were the other provisions more successful, or perhaps it would be fairer to say that they hardly had a fair trial. For the Act had the misfortune to become law in the third month of the War of 1914–18, and during the war period it was tacitly suspended, while the post-war Republican administration had little incentive to enforce it. Thus the interesting experiment of making company directors personally responsible for malpractices committed by their companies remains inconclusive.

The Federal Trade Commission, established by an Act signed in September 1914, had more immediate success. In form it was a non-partisan committee of five members to investigate commercial practices and to issue restraining orders to those who violated the anti-trust laws or engaged in "unfair competition," whose definition was left to the judgment of the Commission, but was held to include such practices as misleading advertising, bribery and adulteration. Its aim was to prevent rather than to punish the commission of offences, and during Wilson's administration it was active in hearing complaints and issuing orders. After 1920, however, the attitude of the administration towards business altered and the Supreme Court in its judgments also reflected the changed climate of opinion. Herbert Hoover, the Secretary of Commerce, encouraged the formation of trade associations and the reports of the Commission were either ignored or failed to get judicial support. The concentration of economic control grew apace, and by 1931 the House of Morgan again controlled, through interlocking directorates, approximately one-quarter of the country's total corporate assets.

The third member of the legislative trio—the Rayburn Securities Act—designed to control the operations of stock exchanges and the manipulation of securities was defeated in the Senate. Its provisions were at length revived in various pieces of legislation passed between 1933 and 1935.

The main impetus of the "New Freedom" at home ended with the Clayton Act. Business was out of breath—a familiar symptom among institutions exposed to Wilson's reforming zeal —and, through House, was suggesting world affairs as a more glorious field for Presidential endeavour. Wilson, too, was tired, naturally absorbed in the new problems created by the European war, and depressed by the death of his wife on August 6th, 1914. Moreover, both he and the Progressives shared the belief that the need for reform was, in a sense, finite, that once competition had been made fair and free, nothing more was needed. This, it seemed, had now been done, and this belief was confirmed by the circumstance that although, in fact, there were still pressure points in the economic system needing relief, these were masked by the rapidly increasing European demand for American goods. By 1915 the adjustment of the American economy to war conditions was complete, the situation began to assume a commercially favourable aspect; the war appeared to many Americans as merely an extension of their export trade. The fact that American production was geared to the needs of a war situation, and particularly after America herself entered the war, gave a new impulse to economic consolidation which the administration was even forced to encourage as facilitating the high degree of governmental control of finance, labour, production and distribution demanded by a war economy.

Yet, if all that had been gained by a frontal

attack on the main American problem was a "painful inch," nevertheless "by creeks and inlets" substantial achievements were registered. Reforming legislation continued into Wilson's second term, and even if it lacked the drama and ambitious scope of the Acts of his first two years, it was perhaps more lasting. The conservation of resources received less attention than might have been expected from the reference to it in his First Inaugural, but the Alaska Railway Act of 1914, empowering the Federal Government to construct, own and operate the Alaskan railroads, guaranteed governmental control of the economic resources of that area beside being a notable incursion into the sacred preserves of private enterprise. The previous neglect of agriculture was redeemed by the Smith-Lever Act of 1914 and the Smith-Hughes Act of 1917, which provided funds for farm demonstration work and agricultural education; it is possible again to discern here the influence of W. H. Page. At sea the La Follette Seamen's Act of 1915 improved conditions in the American Merchant Marine, and in 1916 the government Shipping Board was created to acquire and operate ships. Other Acts established workmen's compensation for Federal Civil Service employees, an eight-hour day on inter-State railways and banned the products of child labour from inter-State commerce.

These would have been notable achievements

for any administration; for a party founded in
the doctrine of State rights and under a leader
whose fundamental belief was not in the maximum of governmental regulation, but in the
minimum of government interference, they were
indeed remarkable. We may echo the judgment
of Morison and Commager:

"All in all, the Democratic party made a
splendid record of intelligent leadership and
harmonious co-operation. They had proved
that progress and statesmanship were not the
monopoly of the Republicans, and that the
progressive movement, which the Populists
had begun and (Theodore) Roosevelt made
popular, transcended party lines."

Wilson's object had been to destroy monopoly
and to maintain free competition as the only
effective instrument of business liberty. To this
end he aimed, on the one hand, to "make crime
personal," and on the other hand, through the
Federal Trade Commission, to inform business
as to what under the law it could and could not
do, to give business a chance to adjust itself to
the new legal prescription before indictment or
prosecution. The establishment of the Federal
Trade Commission is further evidence of the
change which had taken place in Wilson's mind
on two points. First, it showed—as did the establishment of the Tariff Commission—that he had
abandoned his earlier opposition to commissions

as such, as being instruments of tyranny. Second, it showed what again we have noticed in his New Jersey period—a decline in his belief in the ability of the individual to make the adjustments necessary to cure the defects in the contemporary economic system and a rise in his belief that these must come about through governmental machinery. The War of 1914–18 prevented the development of the Commission on the lines intended by Wilson, but his belief in machinery remained and found later expression in the League of Nations Covenant.

Chapter Eight

The New Freedom Abroad

PROBABLY few American Presidents entered office so ambiguously equipped to handle foreign affairs or have been faced as early in their Presidency with so acute problems in that field. Sixteen years of Republican administration had produced an attitude of mind in the State Department not by any means favourable to the Progressivism of Wilson and Bryan. At the same time Bryan was particularly zealous to appoint deserving Democrats, for he was very personal in all his politics and held the pioneer belief that any good man could fill any office, and this led to the introduction of inexperienced men. The administrative confusion in the Department was, in fact, extreme, as the Ambassador to St. James's frequently complained.

Wilson himself had given little attention to foreign relations or to diplomacy; he had studied the machinery whereby a nation maintains itself in peace rather than that by which it pursues war "by other means." On the credit side was the fact that Wilson and Bryan were in agreement on general principles, even if it was felt that Bryan was "too good a Christian to run a naughty world" and that "he does not hate enough." Wilson could be a good hater. Wilson, moreover, came to power believing that the President had virtually absolute control over his country's foreign relations and "may guide every step of diplomacy." Hence he was in no awe of the State Department and quite prepared to cut through the normal relations between it and the corresponding departments of other States, either by sending special envoys to express his views or in other ways. His own diplomatic appointments were certainly up to or even beyond the average of the past, and no country could have wished for better representatives than Walter Hines Page in London, James W. Gerard in Berlin, Brand Whitlock at Brussels or Paul S. Reinsch at Pekin. These, however, were in the Orient or Europe. It was unfortunate that there was no Ambassador of equal calibre in the Western hemisphere until Dwight Morrow went to Mexico in 1927.

The situation which he received from his predecessors was not an enviable one. American policy in the Caribbean and its demand for bases to secure the Panama Canal was the precise counterpart of British policy in the Mediterranean and its dependence on holding Malta and Egypt to secure the Suez Canal. Equally, Roosevelt's "big stick" had caused the U.S.A. to be deeply hated and distrusted in South America, whose principal countries—

Argentina, Brazil and Chile, the so-called ABC Powers—had fought the implications of the Monroe Doctrine for a generation, and had resented Cleveland's action over Venezuela. The policies of Taft and his Secretary of State, Philander Knox, had been stigmatised as "dollar diplomacy."

Wilson had recognised, for example, in his *History of the American People*, that the expansion of American industry and agriculture demanded new markets, to which the Philippines were the threshold, that American Imperialism was providing a new American frontier justifying the "naïve enthusiasm" with which the American people hailed the conquests of their fleets and armies. But when President, he determined to reject "dollar diplomacy" and to repudiate exploitation covered by the Monroe Doctrine, though not the Doctrine itself. He saw abroad the same forces moulding relations between States as moulded, or perverted, relations between citizens—namely, the strength of monopolistic interests. Thus his home and foreign policies were intimately connected and the success or failure of the one implied success or failure of the other. He therefore carried over into his foreign policy *mutatis mutandis* the basic principles of the "New Freedom" which he was seeking to apply at home—faith in morality as the basis of action, a belief in the capacity of peoples to govern themselves once they were educated and in the divine mission of America to broaden the area of world peace and prosperity. This latter was to have a very practical manifestation, for it implied the dissemination of improved conditions of material well-being, demanding in turn the export of American goods and capital which would carry with them into all the world the American way of life, and so generate world peace. None the less, United States nationals trading or investing in foreign countries must no longer expect their country to collect their debts for them or themselves to be immune from the jurisdiction of local courts; further conquests were repudiated, and he desired the Latin-American States as associates in a common policy.

The classical statement of these principles is found in his address at Mobile, Alabama, on October 27th, 1913, to the Southern Commercial Congress. In this he repudiated material interest as a determinant of foreign policy, for "interest does not tie nations together; it sometimes separates them," therefore "it is a spiritual union which we seek." (He repeated this sentiment almost verbatim at Manchester, England, in December 1918.) The aim of America was henceforth to be "the development of constitutional liberty in the world," and "the United States will never seek one additional foot of territory by conquest."

Yet United States Marines continued to keep Nicaragua in the condition of a United States protectorate, while Wilson himself sent troops to Haiti and Santo Domingo and Cuba. Despite his repudiation of Theodore Roosevelt and Taft, he seemed to be continuing their policies. Although he spoke of self-determination and of his desire to conciliate the Latin-American States, dollar diplomacy seemed still to hold the field, a natural consequence of the belief in the need of America for foreign trade which he shared with Knox. But we cannot rule out the Mobile Address as merely diplomatic and hypocritical. There is almost always a time lag between a pronouncement on foreign policy and its becoming effective. It cannot be denied that Wilson's desire that towards Latin-America the United States should act as "their friends and champions upon terms of equality and honour" was sincere and a marked change from the raucous tones of Theodore Roosevelt or that his conduct in his first big test—over Mexico— swayed though it might be by a desire to prevent the British oil interests gaining at the expense of the American, planted a seed of co-operation that was to grow to maturity under the "good neighbor" policy of F. D. Roosevelt and Cordell Hull. Equally, it cannot be denied that the full success of his principles demanded and implied not only the maintenance of peace, but also continuous American leadership in world affairs, neither of which was achieved in Wilson's lifetime, for Europe destroyed the one and America the other.

Before relating Wilson's conduct of the Mexican situation, we may turn to some relatively minor matters which illustrate the strength and weakness of his policy. Taft had approved American participation in a Six-Power loan to China on terms which in Wilson's view endangered Chinese political integrity. Almost his first official act, therefore, was to repudiate American interest in the loan, whereupon the American bankers withdrew. In May he recognised the new Chinese Republic as a way of showing more clearly that the old policy of governmental partnership with international bankers was at an end, whether in the Far East or in South America. This was part of his effort to foster Liberal principles in other lands, but in China he received a setback when the revolt against Yuan Shih Kai led the latter to be as arbitrary as Huerta in Mexico and to give similar reasons for his action. Nor was this the end, for as Japan patently went into the lead in the economic exploitation of China, and especially after 1914, Wilson was driven himself to initiate the formation by American bankers of a Four-Power Consortium for a Chinese loan as a counter-measure.

The increase of Japanese settlement on the West Coast early provided Wilson with a prob-

lem in practical diplomacy, when both the
California and Washington State Legislatures
proposed laws restricting the ownership of property by aliens to those "eligible for citizenship." This action was not inconsistent with
treaty obligations of the United States, but did
cause deep offence to the Japanese government.
Wilson failed to prevent the passage of the legislation proposed, but personal conferences between Bryan and the Japanese Ambassador
managed to keep the two countries at peace
until the issues at stake were submerged by the
onset of the War of 1914. They were, in fact,
never settled

On a related issue Congress overruled
Wilson's veto and passed an Immigration Act in
1917 which ended the traditional free policy of
the United States by excluding numerous classes
of persons. Wilson had previously exercised a
successful veto of an Act imposing on immigrants a test of literacy which might, he argued,
have excluded some of the original Pilgrim
Fathers. Since the war checked immigration,
anyway, the working of the 1917 Act was never
tested, and it was superseded by the Act
of 1921.

A more liberal project of a different sort
which he encouraged was that of Bryan for a
series of bi-lateral treaties whereby the signatories should bind themselves to a preliminary
enquiry into the causes of any dispute before

resorting to war, the period of a year being allowed for such investigation, during which time the disputants would "cool off." This scheme was laid before the diplomats in April 1913, and although received with thinly veiled amusement at home and abroad, Bryan's "grape-juice diplomacy" had, by the end of the year, secured the assent in principle of thirty-one nations, to which number Great Britain was added in January 1914. Germany refused to sign because, as the Kaiser told Colonel House, "Our strength lies in being always prepared for war at a second's notice. We will not resign that advantage and give our enemies time to prepare." In the end twenty-one such treaties were finally concluded, but it must sadly be conceded that they were all fruitless.

We have already referred to the announced intention of the United States to withdraw from the Philippines once a stable government had been established. The Democratic party programme had reaffirmed this. Wilson abolished the Philippine Commission and set up a bi-cameral Legislature based on a popular vote. The Civil Service was staffed increasingly by the Filipinos themselves, and the government, in which the Governor was the sole representative of the power of the United States, established railways, banks, mines and industries under its own control. In his last Message Wilson reminded Congress that the Jones Act of 1916 had promised independence, but the Republican administration which followed him was opposed to its fulfilment. When independence was finally offered by Franklin Roosevelt, it was due less to recollection of the twenty-year-old promise than to sheer material interest. The agricultural and especially the sugar-producing States wished to end the duty-free importation of the products of the islands, American business was disappointed at the failure of the islands to pay the commercial dividends anticipated when they were first annexed, and strategic experts expected that in a war with Japan the islands would be seized by the Japanese anyway. It was a fair illustration of the truth of Wilson's statement at Manchester:

> "Interest separates men. There is only one thing that can bind people together, and that is a common devotion to right."

For whatever self-interest might suggest, the moral obligation proved inescapable.

In 1914 Wilson negotiated a treaty with Colombia expressing regret for the Panama Canal episode and offering 25 million dollars in compensation, Colombia in return to recognise Panama. The Senate twice refused to ratify it, but finally did so in 1921, minus the expression of regret.

A sterner test of Wilson's principles of foreign policy than any of these was provided by events in Mexico. Porfirio Diaz had given the country orderly government at the cost of ruthless suppression of all liberty, oppression of the peons in the interests of a small number of landed proprietors owning enormous acreages and of widespread commercial concessions to American and other nationals. In 1911 he was ousted by the idealistic Francisco Madero, who failed to satisfy the peons or to control the landlords and was himself assassinated in February 1913. He was succeeded by Huerta, described as a short, broad-shouldered man with restless eyes and Indian perseverance, who was said to become more clear-headed the more he drank. During the confusion of the Madero regime it had been suggested to Wilson, when President-elect, that he should consult with the then Secretary of War on a military policy which he could carry out when in power, but Wilson had declined. The Secretary whose overtures were thus rejected was Henry L. Stimson, who was to hold the same office in 1940.

On his assumption of office, Wilson, abandoning the traditional Jeffersonian policy of recognising *de facto* governments, refused to recognise Huerta. This was a bold step, because it was equally opposed to the advice of American industrialists, whose Mexican investments at that time were reckoned at 1,500 million dollars, of American bankers, whose 10 million dollar loan to Mexico matured in June 1913, when a failure to repay would, in their view, compel United States intervention anyway, and of the United States Ambassador in Mexico. Moreover, although Great Britain seemed at first indisposed to recognise Huerta, yet in March, when Wilson appeared committed, she reversed her attitude and decided to recognise him as an "interim President," and this was formally done two months later. In Washington this action was generally regarded, and not least by Bryan and the State Department, as due to the influence of British oil interests, which equally with American were threatened by the Mexican hatred of foreign economic penetration, but saw a chance to undermine the influence of the United States and so safeguard the British Navy's oil supplies.

Wilson, however, held on his course, strengthened by reports from his special envoys, first W. B. Hale and later John Lind, sometime Governor of Minnesota, both of whom shared his Progressive views, a fact which commended their judgment to Wilson, even though neither had any extensive knowledge either of the Spanish language or of Mexican history. As so often before and later, Wilson listened to many voices, but actually took counsel only with himself. He reached the conclusion—by no means a faulty one—that the situation in Mexico was not a mere personal struggle between rival dictators, but was a struggle of the Mexican people to be free from their feudal overlords. The problem, therefore, was less one of constitutional law and of the claim of rival governments to recognition than one of how to serve the best interests of Mexico, the welfare of her people and the encouragement of democratic institutions. To these ends neither the recognition of the latest President who had murdered his predecessor nor armed intervention would serve. He believed, as he told Congress, in the "steady pressure of moral force," and it was a great achievement on Wilson's part that he managed to stay at peace with Mexico. He saw that the interests of the United States also would be best served by a stable government in Mexico, and he rightly declined to believe that one could be achieved under such men as Huerta.

His policy he described in October 1913 to the somewhat startled Sir William Tyrrell, of the Foreign Office, then visiting Washington, in the words, "I am going to teach the South American Republics to elect good men." He had, in August, proposed that elections be held in Mexico at which Huerta should not be a candidate, but Huerta did not accept this suggestion, and, in fact, was himself elected at elections held in October, leaving Wilson with no other resource than "watchful waiting." The only gleam of light was that in July Colonel House had gone to London and explained the aims of Wilson's policy to Sir Edward Grey, the British

Foreign Secretary, who had listened sympathetically. That such a move was necessary showed the paucity of contacts between the State Department and the Foreign Office, a fact of some significance because the final agreement, whereby the British withdrew recognition from Huerta, was reached in such private conversations as those of House in London and Sir William Tyrrell in Washington, and could hardly be described as "open covenants openly arrived at."

In February 1914 the situation flared up when Wilson decided to lift the embargo which he had hitherto maintained on the exportation of arms to Mexico. This he did with the view of assisting the Constitutionalist party, under Carranza. The reaction in the United States was favourable, but in Mexico an American naval crew was arrested at Tampico on April 9th, and two days later further arrests took place at Vera Cruz. The American Admiral Mayo promptly, and without consulting either the Navy or State Departments in Washington, issued an ultimatum demanding an apology, and ten days later Vera Cruz was seized, partly as a sanction and partly to prevent the landing there of munitions coming in a German ship and intended for Huerta. Admiral Mayo may have hoped to force the abdication of Huerta, but actually Carranza as well as Huerta protested at his action, which, as Secretary of the Navy Josephus Daniels has dryly pointed out, neither procured the apology nor prevented the munitions from reaching Huerta, for the German ship steamed quietly on to another port.

From this position of difficulty Wilson was now rescued by the ABC Powers, who on April 25th, 1914, made an offer of mediation, which was accepted, the Senate Foreign Relations Committee and Senator Lodge concurring. Representatives of the Powers met at Niagara Falls, traditional resort of honeymoon couples, and Wilson hoped for a complete settlement, including the elimination of Huerta and a provisional government acceptable to all parties. In June an agreement was reached on a provisional government, but this was not signed by the Carranzistas, nor was anything said about internal reforms. Nevertheless, Britain at this time withdrew her recognition of Huerta, who, finding himself deserted on all sides, resigned in July and fled the country. In August Carranza entered Mexico City. This was regarded in the United States as a triumph for the Wilsonian method, and the result even won some approval in Europe, while relations with Latin-America were improved by the evidence of the pacific and co-operative disposition of the great Republic of the North.

Wilson, however, with somewhat greater prescience, saw the situation as merely a clearing of the stage, and in this he was right, for civil

war broke out again when Villa drove Carranza
from the capital. Again the ABC Powers, now
reinforced by Uruguay and Guatemala, met to
work out a settlement, but not until October
1915 did Carranza regain control and receive
recognition as the *de facto* ruler of Mexico. In
March of the following year, however, Villa
raided New Mexico. Wilson sent Brigadier-
General John J. Pershing to catch him, but Villa
eluded capture and threatened further raids, so
that eventually some 150,000 men were patrol-
ling the frontier. Wilson firmly refused to
invade Mexico or to agree to annexation,
although strongly pressed by American property-
owners, Roman Catholics and his political
opponents, representative of the old American
Imperialism. He continued his attempts to get
Mexico's house in order, and a joint commission
of United States and Mexican representatives
did reach agreement in November 1916. At the
end of the year, however, Carranza denounced
the agreement, and Wilson then had to leave the
situation alone. He recognised that the basic
difficulty was Mexican suspicion of the intentions of the United States, which dated from
the seizure of Texas in 1845. He hoped, in time,
to convince Mexico that American intervention
in the affairs of South American Republics was
a passing phase, and that she would not in the
future take advantage of weak Powers. In the
meantime further involvement in Mexican

affairs would be merely a distraction, operating increasingly in favour of Germany, with whom relations were getting more and more strained. In time Mexico acquired a certain stability as Carranza made some agrarian reforms to satisfy the land-hunger of the peasants, which was one of the main causes of revolution. He was assassinated in 1920 and succeeded by Obregon, who signed a treaty with the United States in 1923.

If Mexico tried Wilson's patience, his handling of the Panama Canal Tolls showed his honesty. The Hay-Pounceforte Treaty of 1901 between Great Britain and the United States had clearly stipulated that canal charges on ships of all nations should be the same. Nevertheless, in 1912 the Canal Act had authorised free passage for American coast-wise shipping. In securing equal rights to the use of a canal when she had not shared the expense of building it, British diplomacy was widely held to have "over-reached" that of the United States—and the Canal Act was widely approved in consequence. It had been endorsed in the Democratic platform at Baltimore, and Wilson himself had made one speech in its defence. It was possible to argue that since the Canal Zone was the property of the United States, coast-wise shipping was internal transportation, so that the concession gave the United States no competitive advantage over foreign vessels. But when Wilson came to study the Treaty, he was convinced that it had been broken and that the protests of the British were well founded. On March 5th, 1914, therefore, he asked Congress to repeal the Act. The House of Representatives passed the necessary legislation in the same month, but the Senate was more recalcitrant, and Wilson seriously considered resigning and "taking the matter to the people." In June, however, the Senate, responding to pressure and to the argument of Senator Lodge that they should not discredit the President in a matter of foreign policy, passed an Act of repeal, which Wilson signed on June 15th.

The British reaction was immediately favourable, and Grey gave his opinion that Wilson's action lifted public life on to a higher plane. It was, indeed, a striking demonstration of honesty in international politics and enhanced the reputation of the United States no less than that of Wilson. It also demonstrated Wilson's power over Congress, even at the end of his first year, always an awkward time for Presidents.

In his Message recommending the repeal of the Canal Act, Wilson had referred to the assistance that such action would give him in other matters of high policy. By many this was taken as indicating a private understanding with Great Britain on reciprocal action in Mexico, and this view was strengthened when Britain promptly withdrew recognition from Huerta and generally followed Wilson's lead in Mexican affairs. Actually, however, it seems that Wilson had wider problems in mind, and designed the repeal of the Canal Act to smooth the way for a visit to Europe by Colonel House in the interests of peace and reduction of armaments which he had planned for the summer of 1914.

Chapter Nine

America Enters the War

PRIOR to his inauguration, Wilson's personal knowledge of Europe had been limited to a couple of visits to Great Britain, where he had spent his time chiefly in Scotland and the Lake District, following his interests in poetry and education rather than in politics, in which he was, in any case, more concerned with domestic than with foreign issues. In so far as he had considered external affairs, and particularly in the few months intervening between his election as President and his assumption of office, it was to the Western Hemisphere that he had turned his mind. Thus the various international alarms in Europe, Algeciras, Agadir, the Balkan Wars and the Anglo-German naval race, made so little impression on him that in his first Annual Message to Congress of December 1913 he was able to say,

"Many happy manifestations multiply about us of a growing cordiality and sense of unity of interest among the nations, foreshadowing an era of settled peace and goodwill."

More percipient than Wilson, or perhaps more ambitious, Colonel House desired that the

United States should develop towards Europe as well as towards Latin-America a foreign policy more positive than the general philanthropy of Bryan and his arbitration treaties, and in this he was at one with Page, the American Ambassador in London. The traditional dislike of the United States for foreign alliances was certainly an obstacle, but House hoped to bring about a naval agreement between England and Germany, and to draw the Great Powers into some general understanding for the development and protection of backward regions.

With these ideas in his mind, with Wilson's blessing and the Panama Tolls controversy happily ended, he set off for Europe in May 1914. But while Wilson appreciated that the settlement of the Canal controversy would smooth House's path, there is very little evidence that he applied his mind to the problems or suggestions which House put forward. Indeed, the opposite is almost certainly the case. Domestic affairs and Mexico were sufficient occupation for Wilson, who himself admitted that he had "a single-track mind" and preferred to tackle only one problem at a time. House's idea to give Germany a "zone of influence" in Asia Minor and Persia would hardly have appealed to Wilson's dislike of "Imperialism," and although his messages to House in Europe were extremely cordial and affectionate, they did not contain any indication that he himself seriously considered the letters from House to which he was supposed to be replying. Had he done so, he could hardly have failed to see the dubious logic of House's conclusion that France's failure to keep step with Germany's growing population would incline her to accept the *status quo* and to give up the idea of revenge or recovery of Alsace-Lorraine.

The aggressive militarism of Berlin was a great shock to House, but his letters to Wilson maintained their vein of optimism. On June 26th he wrote encouragingly about his plan for joint action by the United States, Great Britain, France and Germany to safeguard and encourage investment in the "waste places of the earth" which he had discussed in London and Berlin. There is some doubt as to whether Wilson ever received this letter, for House apparently sent a further copy on July 4th, and by this time an Austrian Archduke had already been assassinated at Sarajevo. Two days after House sailed for home Germany declared war on Russia.

The outbreak of war took Wilson by surprise, and his first reaction was of irritation at an apparently senseless interruption to his programme of domestic reform. Owing to its chronic lack of information, the State Department seems to have been taken equally unawares. Both, indeed, had their several distractions. The autumn of 1914 would see the mid-term Congressional elections, and Bryan, like the political warhorse he was, had smelt the election from afar, and was busy speech-making in the Middle West. Wilson was preoccupied in watching the first-fruits of his reform legislation, and notably the start of the Federal Reserve System. Moreover, the end of July and early August was overshadowed by personal tragedy. He conscientiously carried out the duties of his office, but while the strain of his wife's illness and her death on August 6th did not perhaps affect his judgment of the international situation, it did certainly dull the clarity with which he sought to give effect to that judgment.

Admittedly his great successor twenty-five years later was to be no more successful with offers of mediation, but equally Wilson's lacked the directness of Franklin Roosevelt's, being either couched in general terms or advanced through intermediaries. That he should at once proclaim American neutrality was inevitable. Wilson had seen the wreckage and ruin of war in the South, and knew what it was like, and, despite the evidence of the Civil War, profoundly disbelieved in the power of war to settle disputed questions. Moreover, besides causing loss of life, war "is autocratic," and would lead to a dependence on Big Business which would endanger the reforms which he had carried through during the preceding two years. He therefore urged his countrymen to be "impartial in thought as well as in action," and to show themselves "a Nation that neither sits in judgment upon others nor is disturbed in her own counsels."

At this distance of time it is all too easy to poke fun at these aspirations, and, indeed, two years later Wilson himself was to say, "This is the last war of its kind or of any kind that involves the world that the United States can keep out of. The business of neutrality is over." But at the time it could be definitely argued that no practical means existed for American intervention in Belgium (the 1914 counterpart of 1939 Poland), while nowhere in the United States was public opinion prepared for intervention, even had it appeared practicable. For this reason alone—and it was not the only one—American neutrality was inevitable.

But we may fairly criticise Wilson on two points: first, for a lack of realism in appealing for impartiality in thought when, as an historian if not as President, he must have been aware of the strength of racial feeling in a country drawn, as he said in the self-same Message, "from many nations and chiefly from the nations now at war." Second, while it was true that neither Wilson nor his country was ever apt to be disturbed in their own counsels, it was naïve, in view of the record in the Caribbean, Mexico and South America generally, to claim that they never sat in judgment upon others. Still, although House thought that Wilson lacked appreciation of the full significance of the European crisis and had missed a chance to lay down a positive policy in foreign affairs, Wilson's stand, and his way of expressing it, won general support, not only in the country at large, but from public men of all parties—from President C. W. Eliot of Harvard, who on reconsideration withdrew his proposal that America should forthwith join the Allies, from ex-Presidents Theodore Roosevelt and Taft, and from Senator Lodge, although he later stigmatised Wilson's position as unsound, and therefore impracticable.

At least his position was difficult not merely to maintain, but even to define, for such international law or conventions as might cover the rights of neutrals were either not universally accepted or had failed to keep pace with such developments in the technique of war as the use of submarines and wireless stations, or with the new significance of cotton, copper and even foodstuffs, as war materials. There was thus an inevitable divergence between the American government, which sincerely desired to be politically neutral, but could only invoke the outworn conventions of the nineteenth century, and American industry, which desired to meet the needs of both belligerents for war materials of all kinds and was therefore bound to become economically entangled in the European struggle, no matter what Washington or Jefferson had said. The basic position common to both was that no foreign Power should be allowed to interfere with the trading rights of Americans, and thus while Wilson was prepared to exert his powers of leadership and to guide industry and finance in domestic matters, in foreign economic relationships he was constrained to allow bankers and industrialists to operate freely. War material was not embargoed, and although in August loans to belligerents were frowned on by the American Treasury, by October they were permitted in the guise of commercial credits.

There were, indeed, economic reasons, both general and particular, behind this desire for the utmost freedom of wartime trade. A general reason was foreshadowed by Wilson in his Acceptance Speech of 1912, when he said that the industries of the country "have expanded to such a point they will burst their jackets if they cannot find a free outlet to the markets of the world." Even earlier he had seen this expansion as explaining the development of the American Empire in the late nineteenth century. It is worth remembering also that before the First World War the United States was on balance a debtor country to whom the free sale of her goods abroad was essential. From this point of view the European penchant for autumn declarations of war produced a most unfortunate situation in that it was at this season of the year that the balances held abroad against the United States, and particularly in London, were dangerously high. Normally they would have been liquidated by shipments of wheat, cotton and tobacco, and the coincidence of the declaration of war with the American cotton harvest exercised particular pressure on the Administration to insist on neutral rights to trade with both belligerents. Southern agriculture, which did not look to benefit from the trade in armaments, saw cotton prices falling from $13\frac{1}{2}$ cents per lb. in 1913 to from 6–$6\frac{1}{2}$ cents in August 1914. Moreover, the diversion of so much of the British and German Merchant Marine on which America relied portended a catastrophic loss of foreign commerce which would affect not only the private interests of merchants, bankers and railroads, but also the returns from tariffs and taxation.

Wilson and McAdoo were prompt to accept the responsibility of leadership, and proposed to meet the economic crisis by three measures—the formation of a "cotton loan fund" to enable the Southern farmers to hold their surplus crops, the building by the government of merchant ships and the prevention of cotton being declared contraband. The first of these measures was carried without difficulty, but the proposal for a government-owned corporation to buy and build ships was violently opposed by the shipping interests, who had no desire to curtail the

very profitable conjunction of a shortage of
freight with a reduction of British and German
competition under the protection of government
war-risk insurance. The Republican politicians
also saw a chance to attack Wilson's leadership,
and the prospect of further extensions of executive power if the war continued. Thus, although
Wilson strongly supported the scheme in a
bellicose and colloquial speech on Jackson Day
(January 8th), 1915, and the House of Representatives passed the necessary legislation,
proceedings were held up by a filibuster in the
Senate, and Congress adjourned on March 4th
with nothing done.

The dispute over the Shipping Bill had gone
deep into questions of economic privilege and
raised personal animosities which smouldered
for the next four years. It may be said to mark
the inevitable check in Wilson's first flood of
success which we have noticed before at Princeton and at Trenton. From now on Congressional
resistance grew in strength, while Wilson himself ceased to regard Congress, and the Senate in
particular, as colleagues. Politics began to return
to their traditional pattern of mutual rivalry
between the Legislature and the Executive.

The question of cotton contraband will serve
as a key to the disputes with Great Britain
during the next two and a half years, disputes
which turned on questions of international law.
Their detailed description would take up too

much space, but the issues may be briefly set out.

In 1909 the delegates of ten countries had signed the Declaration of London, which aimed at safeguarding the rights of neutral traders in time of war, but because the British government had not ratified it the Declaration had not become operative by August 4th, 1914. It was, however, a natural move for the American government to propose on August 6th that the belligerents should regulate their actions by this document. Germany and Austria at once agreed, subject to acceptance by the Allies, for this would ensure that supplies of essential commodities would not be cut off by naval blockade. Precisely for this reason the British government would not agree to the proposal, except with such modifications as would render the Declaration powerless to restrain the drastic employment of British sea power, for Britain was concerned to prevent trade not only with her enemies, but also with Continental neutrals through whom supplies might pass, and was prepared to justify the interruption of trade between neutrals by invoking the doctrine of "continuous voyage."

Since it was manifestly impossible to convince the British government that adherence to the Declaration of London would not cripple the effectiveness of the British Fleet, Lansing, in Bryan's absence, could only invoke the provisions of international law as they stood prior to the attempted codification of 1909. This task was, however, made almost equally impossible by the precedents established during the Civil War by the Federal government itself, which had rigorously blockaded the South and invoked the doctrine of "continuous voyage." To put pressure on the Allies by an embargo on their purchases would have violated the rights of belligerents to trade with neutrals, and would thus have been an un-neutral act. Besides, the disruption of normal trade made the United States economically dependent on Allied military purchases, and Wilson could not afford to overlook this in the autumn of a mid-term election year. In any event, he had no desire to find himself in a situation like that of Madison (also a Princeton man) in 1812, when the United States drifted into and out of war with England on very similar grounds.

Lansing therefore, on October 22nd, was forced to abandon the effort to enforce the Declaration of London. Britain at once released a number of cargoes held up in British ports pending determination of this issue, and three days later declared that she would not regard cotton as contraband of war. Other assurances designed to conciliate the South were also given, but in practice they proved of little value, and in August 1915, as it became safe to ignore the political influence of the South, cotton was replaced on the contraband list.

Interference by the Allies with American trade, in fact, continued, leading to protests, which Page presented unwillingly to Grey and not infrequently helped him to answer. By a British public which could never realise that America was not predominantly Anglo-Saxon, but was, in fact, pervaded with anti-British sentiment, these protests were received with contemptuous irritation, while the Foreign Office fully appreciated the weakness of the American position. For while the State Department might continue to protest at Allied illegalities, it could not overlook the fact that if trade were stopped and a serious conflict with Britain developed, it would be disastrous to the American economic system. Indeed, more than that. For while in 1913 American industrial output was of the order of 20 thousand million dollars and foreign trade about 2 thousand million dollars, by 1917 output had increased to 30 thousand million dollars and foreign trade to 6 thousand million dollars, while the United States had repaid its European debts and was a creditor nation with a large gold reserve.

So an understanding was gradually built up whereby under certain safeguards the imports of Continental neutrals were rationed, while American producers could obtain embargoed commodities upon giving an undertaking not to export products manufactured from them to destinations to which Britain objected. Meanwhile, in March 1915, the American government finally withdrew its opposition to the granting of credits to belligerents by American banks.

The arrangement enabled the Allies steadily to tighten the blockade of Germany while continuing to enjoy free access to American commerce. This was of vital importance, and it involves no disparagement of the valour of the American Army to suggest that the final outcome of the war was determined less by their participation in the campaigns of 1918 than by Wilson's decisions during the period of American neutrality which governed the disposition of American goods and money.

Since Germany, by this policy, was deprived of her hope to break the blockade by legal means, she might resort to measures of retaliation which would lead to war with the United States. This ultimately happened, but to see just why the United States finally declared war on Germany and not on the Allies, we must go back again to 1914.

When war broke out, Wilson condemned both sides equally for starting a war which, as late as October 1916, he was to say was caused, in his view, by nothing in particular. This attitude was partly a reflection of his determination to be impartial, partly the result of definite lack of information, due in its turn to the conditions in the State Department already noted, to Wilson's own inability to cope with and analyse the mass of papers reaching his desk and to his reliance on House, whose reports were superficial. As time went on, however, Wilson appeared to be less concerned with the responsibility for the war and more with the manner in which it was being waged, and with its possible outcome. This last point, indeed, was in his mind from the start, and his desire to mediate between the combatants and to bring the war to an early close was strongly supported by Bryan, who urged in September that neither side was likely to be able in the end to dictate terms, while if either side did so, this would merely lay the foundations for the next war.

Bryan seems to have seen more clearly than most the dangers which must follow the attempt of the President to insist on strict observance of neutral rights, and alone of the Administration he urged a constructive policy for avoiding them. He suggested various proposals, some of which had already been broached by Wilson—for example, guarantees of territorial integrity and a government monopoly of munitions—and others which Wilson himself was to revive in the winter of 1916, when it was too late. At this time, when, as House later admitted, peace parleys might have been effective, Bryan's appeals went unheard, for Wilson favoured House's plan for a personal mission, and moves towards peace were postponed during the discussion on the Declaration of London, whose outcome encouraged Britain in her belief in eventual victory.

Thus it was not until the end of January 1915 that House sailed in the *Lusitania* "in a blaze of mystery," arriving in London on February 6th. But even in London he tarried, seduced, so it was believed, by the charm and subtlety of Grey and the British, so that by the time he reached Berlin the opportune moment had passed, and his quest for peace merely established the unwillingness of either belligerent to yield. Indeed, two days before House reached Berlin, the Germans had declared the waters around Great Britain a zone in which enemy ships would be sunk without precautions for the safety of those on board, and even neutrals would be in danger because of alleged misuse by the British of neutral flags.

The American reply, worked out by Lansing and Wilson, was that such action was contrary to the recognised rules of war and that the German government would be held to a "strict accountability" for the loss of any American lives or ships. To show American public opinion that the President was definitely neutral, a simultaneous protest was made to Great Britain on the use of neutral flags, but neither protest produced any result, and all immediate hope of American mediation between Great Britain and Germany was destroyed by the torpedoing of the

Lusitania on May 7th, 1915, the fourth in a series of sinkings in which American lives were lost.

To House and Page in London, and to many others on both sides of the Atlantic, it appeared that a declaration of war on Germany must surely follow. Indeed even to-day the belief exists that America entered the First World War to avenge the sinking of the *Lusitania*. But in Washington Congress, which alone can declare war, was not in session, and Wilson did not think that his position as trustee for the people required him to proceed to the extremity of asking for a declaration of war, the full implications of which they would not understand. He believed that the United States should continue to seek peace and ensue it as a positive elevating influence in the world, not just for the sake of avoiding war, but as a sign of self-control and self-mastery. This is the burden of his speech at Philadelphia on May 10th, 1915, in which he used the phrase "Too proud to fight," a phrase as unfairly used by critics as the equally famous "Wait and see" of Asquith. Faced with the choice between breaking off diplomatic relations as a preliminary to war and demanding prompt disavowal and assurances for the future from the German government, Wilson decided on the latter course, a choice that was generally commended at the time by his own nation. Even in England, calmer judgment was inclined to prefer that America should remain a provider of the munitions of war rather than become an active participant who would need munitions herself.

Wilson's first *Lusitania* Note went right to the heart of the matter when he pointed out the manifest impossibility for a submarine to conform to the existing rules of war, since it could not surface to give warning to an enemy vessel and allow time for those on board to disembark, or to put on board a prize crew, without exposing itself to danger of being destroyed. But he could hardly expect Germany to accept his corollary that submarine warfare must be given up, since it was their sole weapon against the British blockade and, as time was to show, by no means an ineffective one. Here lay the crucial difficulty of the German position—viz., that where her situation seemed to require her to break existing international law, she could only do so at the cost of human lives, while Britain's breaches of existing law only involved the seizure of property.

The weakness of the American position lay in the fact that it was grounded on legal concepts which had been rendered obsolete by subsequent technical developments, and that she was unwilling either to revise the law or put her views to the test of force. Of the last point the Germans were aware through a conversation between Bryan and Dumba, the Austrian

Ambassador, duly reported to Berlin, in which Bryan intimated that there was no need to take seriously the American protests. He did, in fact, want Wilson to send some unofficial communication to this effect. The Germans therefore continued to answer Wilson evasively, and particularly since, with Hindenburg's successful attack on Russia, the land war seemed to be going well. Both Wilson's first and second *Lusitania* Notes, in which he insisted alike on international law and on principles of humanity, satisfied the mass of the American nation, but though the concluding words of the second Note were almost an ultimatum, its most tangible result was the resignation of Bryan, who disapproved of its threatening tone. For once, however, the country seemed out of sympathy with Bryan, and his action was not supported. The appointment of Robert Lansing made little difference in policy, which continued to be determined by Wilson. By July Wilson evidently felt that the controversy had lost much of its edge and that the Germans were prepared to modify their methods.

Although the *Lusitania* case remained unsettled until the close of the war, in September, following the sinking of the *Arabic*, the German government did give assurances that liners would not be sunk without warning, provided they did not resist. Such as it was, this was a diplomatic victory, but the sinking of the

Hesperian three days later led Wilson to wonder whether Germany would ever keep faith with anyone. He was being ground between the upper and nether millstones—the growing bellicosity of Theodore Roosevelt and the permanent pacifism of Bryan—and Britain took advantage of this moment to declare cotton to be absolute contraband (August 1915). Despite this, however, during the summer and autumn of 1915 Wilson's sympathies were clearly veering to the Allied side. He was no longer "neutral in thought," though still insisting on the need to control his natural emotions until public opinion was fully formed.

After the third *Lusitania* Note, which, while firm, needed no other answer than the maintenance by Germany of right conduct in the future, he dropped further discussion and turned his attention to national defence, on which he had already had discussions with the Secretaries of War and the Navy. His first concrete proposals, set out in a speech on November 4th, 1915, provided for an armed force of 400,000 soldiers receiving annual training, partly in the National Guard, for a period of three years. Increased naval development was also proposed. These proposals satisfied neither extreme of opinion as represented by Roosevelt and Bryan, but they roused no particular excitement until, under the slogan of "Preparedness," the problem became one element in party manœuvring for the 1916 Presidential election. A demand for universal military service was started by Theodore Roosevelt and the Republicans, and Senator George E. Chamberlain, Democrat, of Oregon, took up the cry. Lindley Garrison, Secretary of War, was also persuaded, but Wilson, after a tour through New York, Missouri and Kansas to test and mould public feeling (as always, he regarded opposition as due to uninformed public opinion, which would turn to him once it became informed), decided not to support Garrison, who resigned, to be succeeded by Newton D. Baker, as avowed a pacifist as Bryan. By taking part in a Preparedness Parade in Washington, D.C., Wilson took the political sting out of the agitation, and during the summer a National Defence Act was passed raising the regular Army to 175,000, giving the President, in the event of war, sundry powers—for example, over the railroads—and authorising a programme of increased naval construction.

It may well be contended that such modest measures were hardly adequate to the situation, for in February the Germans had announced that they would treat all armed merchantmen as warships, and in March had sunk the *Sussex*, an unarmed cross-Channel passenger steamer not following any of the troop or supply routes. Since the British would not renounce their right to arm merchant ships nor the Germans withdraw their proclamation, the deadlock seemed complete.

At this point two Democratic members of Congress—Gore in the Senate, and McLemore in the House of Representatives—introduced identical Resolutions that Americans be warned not to travel on belligerent ships. This advice, which seemed reasonable to Americans during the next war, seemed to Wilson an encroachment on the rights of citizens and a deliberate abdication of his country's position as "spokesman, even amid the turmoil of war, for the Law and the Right." He therefore threw the weight of his influence against the Gore/McLemore Resolution and was able to secure its defeat, in all the circumstances an outstanding political victory. In the case of the *Sussex* he was able to claim a diplomatic victory, for the German reply to the American Note, although mostly taken up with complaints at the illegal conduct of the Allies, made an indubitable concession to Wilson's demand that merchant vessels should not be sunk without warning, which sufficed to prevent a rupture with Germany for nine months.

Such a rupture was, in fact, being prepared by Colonel House, who in December had propounded a scheme whereby the President, at a moment to be signified by the Allies, should invite the belligerents to a Peace Conference proposing terms which it was known or assumed that Germany would not accept. On her refusal, the United States would then enter the war against her. House believed that he had secured the agreement of Grey, but Wilson, in agreeing to the draft of the plan, inserted the word "probably" in the clause committing the United States to enter the war on the Allied side. This was certainly no more than a recognition by Wilson that it is Congress, and not the President, which declares war, and though the defeat of the Gore/McLemore Resolution might indicate that his control of Congress was complete, the element of doubt that was thereby introduced seems to have been enough to prevent the Allies from giving to Colonel House the long-awaited signal.

Another interesting event in this highly charged pre-election summer was the appearance of Wilson and Senator Lodge at a meeting, on May 27th, of the League to Enforce Peace. Although the political relations between the two men were by no means friendly, on this occasion their speeches were curiously in agreement. Lodge vindicated the need to put force behind international peace, and argued that Washington's famous warning was not to be taken as forbidding the United States to join other civilised nations in diminishing war and encouraging peace. Wilson in his turn advocated a universal association of nations to maintain the freedom of the seas and to guarantee territorial

integrity and political independence. When the
latter guarantee turned up again as Article X of
the Covenant of the League of Nations, Lodge
was to oppose it vehemently. But in May 1916
both speakers had their eye on the forthcoming
election. Thus, their advocacy on this occasion
of international pacification, combined with
preparedness and national defence, was an
attempt to secure a political Athanasian Creed
within which whoever wished to vote would
find all that was necessary for his political
salvation.

For the election of 1916 was as critical both
for the United States and for the world as that
of 1940. On the Democratic side Wilson was the
only possible candidate, although hated by the
party leaders because of his conscientious opposition to vested interests. He was the best
Democratic spokesman since Andrew Jackson,
and if the election were fought on domestic
issues, he could appeal with considerable effect
to an unexampled record of legislative achievement. But it was inevitable that it should be
fought on foreign policy, and European policy
at that, which Elihu Root had tersely and not
too inaccurately described as being that of "a
government that shakes its fist first and its finger
afterwards." However, so far America had not
been drawn into the conflict, and at the Democratic Convention in St. Louis in June Wilson's
nomination was supported by the argument "He

kept us out of war," which henceforward was the slogan of the Democratic campaign.

As a slogan it had several advantages—it was strictly accurate as a statement of fact, and it left the Republicans with an apparent choice between an advocacy of war and an advocacy of nothing. Wilson, however, must have realised the fallacy of assuming that it carried any promise for the future, for he had become convinced at least a year earlier that ultimate American participation was inevitable. Yet were he to come out for war, he would inevitably be defeated, and all hope of completing his domestic reforms would be scrapped. The most he could do was by his Preparedness programme to make a feeble gesture towards those sections of the country which demanded stronger measures than diplomacy alone could produce, although even in this sphere he could claim considerable success, as in the *Sussex* affair.

Moreover, there was now no split in the Republican ranks as there had been four years previously. The Progressives had been steadily vanishing since 1914, for Wilson had substantially carried out their policy. They were no longer strong enough to set up a separate party, nor even strong enough to secure the nomination of Theodore Roosevelt. They were just strong enough to prevent the nomination of either Senators Root or Lodge, and thus as a compromise the Republican Convention at

Chicago nominated Chief Justice Charles E.
Hughes. On the diplomatic issue Hughes confined himself to saying that he stood
unflinchingly for the maintenance of all rights
of American citizens on land or sea, and when
asked what line he would have taken over the
Lusitania merely coughed. A candidate of less
personal honesty might have managed some
more impressive reply, but of all the Republicans Hughes was probably nearest to Wilson
in character, and perhaps even in policy—any
difference was no greater than that between
Wendell Willkie and Franklin D. Roosevelt in
1940. But although the party was not evidently
splitting, it was in a state of inner tension
between the pro-German wing of La Follette,
the violent anti-German tirades of Theodore
Roosevelt and the Radical elements of the
former Progressive party. It was therefore bound
to be non-committal on foreign affairs. Nevertheless, the Germans had some reason for their
belief that Hughes would take a stronger line
against Britain than Wilson had done, and for
regarding the possible re-election of Wilson as a
blow to their cause.

This is what made the election a critical one,
quite apart from the fact that again the traditional lines were drawn of the industrial North
against the South and West. The result was
extraordinarily close. Indeed, Wilson went to
bed on the night of November 7th believing that

Hughes had been elected, and only learnt in the morning that the Western votes, and particularly those of California, had finally swung the balance in his favour.

Re-elected thus in virtue of his pacific policy, Wilson continued his efforts to compose the struggle, becoming daily more bitter. In October he had expressed the view that the war was caused by "nothing in particular." In December the Germans sent a peace message, asking Wilson to call a conference of the combatants, as a preliminary to which the Allies were to lay down their arms. Wilson's reply was given in a speech on December 18th, when he stated that, judging by the public statements made by governments, the objects of the statesmen on both sides were virtually the same. He therefore asked both sides to publish the terms on which they would be willing to end the war. Doubtless he hoped that the Allies, whose situation appeared precarious, would return a moderate reply which could serve as a basis for discussion. But they remained firm in their demand for the evacuation of Belgium, while the Germans, who apparently saw themselves as indubitably destined for victory, spoke of retaining Belgium and of indemnities, with German control from Berlin to Baghdad.

Despite the patent irreconcilability of these points of view, on January 22nd, 1917, Wilson made one last offer of mediation in an Address to the Senate, in which he urged that the only durable peace would be "a peace without victory." It must be agreed that such a view sprang from great fortitude of mind, which could see beyond the circumstances of the immediate present, but to the combatants it rather appeared to connote a stark insensibility to the realities of politics and of war. The German reply at least was prompt and brusque. On January 31st she declared unrestricted submarine warfare and a complete blockade of Europe, except for one American ship weekly, which was to carry prescribed merchandise and follow a prescribed route. The Germans evidently counted on a quick victory, and apparently supposed that even so gross a breach as this of the pledge given after the *Sussex* incident would not rouse Wilson to action. For the *Sussex* pledge had kept the peace with the United States for nine months. Had German diplomacy been equal to playing a waiting game, this period might have been prolonged, with who knows what consequences for the final outcome of the war.

Even as it was, the breach of diplomatic relations on February 3rd did not lead to an immediate declaration of war. This was partly due to the fact that as war came evidently closer, Wilson's mental uncertainty and distress increased, reaching a climax on the eve of the declaration itself. But also, paradoxically enough, the election had weakened his hold on Congress, making the Republicans recalcitrant and the Democrats likely to bolt. This was shown in February, when his demand for wider powers and particularly for authority to arm merchant ships, together with other important Bills and appropriations, was defeated by a Senatorial filibuster led by O'Gorman, representing the New York Irish, La Follette the German Swedes of Wisconsin, Stone the Germans of Missouri and Norris of Nebraska, a Bryanite Pacifist. Wilson's relations with the Senate were not improved by a stinging message to the press, in which he condemned the action of this "little group of willful men," the Senate resenting the implied condemnation of their whole body. Such an attitude on the part of Congress reinforced Wilson's reluctance to ask for a declaration of war until Germany had proceeded to "overt acts."

Undoubtedly the American people was confused by this rupture of diplomatic relations while remaining at peace, and Wilson did nothing to ease their confusion or give them the clear leadership that he had hitherto regarded as his duty and they had come to expect. British Naval Intelligence contributed to the clarification of public opinion by sending to the State Department on February 26th a copy of a Note signed by Zimmerman, the German Chancellor, to the German Ambassador in Mexico, in which the latter was instructed to offer Arizona, Texas and New Mexico if Mexico should join Germany in attacking the United States. The State Department published the Note on March 1st, and public opinion hardened against Germany. On March 4th Wilson took the oath for his second term of office, and in his Inaugural Address pointed out the tasks awaiting the United States on the world stage and in collaboration with the "wide and universal forces of mankind," using a memorable phrase, "We are provincials no longer."

During March three merchant vessels were sunk, and by the end of the month Wilson had concluded that there was no alternative to a declaration of war—"What else can I do?" he exclaimed despairingly. On April 2nd he called Congress into special session to hear a message recommending a declaration of war, which was voted on April 6th.

Why, then, did the United States enter the war? Not, at least not directly, to avenge the American lives lost in the *Lusitania*, nor primarily, as was suggested by American Liberals, to safeguard the credits which the House of Morgan had negotiated for the Allies. The root of the matter was that, although both belligerents had been violating the rights of the United States, there was this significant difference, that in order to win the war Germany had to sink ships, Britain needed only to stop them.

Britain, that is to say, was only violating United States property rights, which could be vindicated by a claim for damages, while Germany was taking human lives. Yet for the first two years of the war Wilson, in public at least, professed to see little to choose between the two sides, his opinion of the Allies being not a little influenced by the fact that they included Czarist Russia, regarded as a land of despotic tyranny. The Russian Revolution of 1917, which was warmly welcomed at the time by Americans, contributed powerfully to change this opinion and helped to ease Wilson's adherence to a cause which he could now regard unreservedly as that of democracy.

For to Wilson the war appeared chiefly as a continuation on a wider stage of the struggle against interests and privilege which he had waged successively at Princeton, in New Jersey and in the nation as a whole; it was for the United States, free from motives of aggrandisement, to turn from reforming abuses at home to preventing the abuses abroad which would result from a victory of German Imperialism, compounded as it was of militarism, industry and finance. Wilson had always seen life in terms of service; the individual finding his fullest development in the service of the community, the university in the service of the nation, the nation in the service of humanity. To preserve his countrymen for this service had been his

227

object in maintaining neutrality; to lead them into it was the keynote of his request to Congress for a declaration of war; to keep them in it was to be his vision in the making of peace.

Chapter Ten

America Leaves the Peace

DURING his Governorship of New Jersey, Wilson had confided to his secretary, Joseph Tumulty, his fears that the next President would have a war on his hands, and his doubts as to whether he himself would make a good War President. In the event these doubts proved unjustified. A variety of emotions, ranging from disappointment at the failure of American neutrality to indignation at Germany's breach of a solemn pledge, united to arouse the Scots Covenanting pugnacity that was ever dormant in Wilson. Although he continued to explore avenues of peace, at the same time there was no hesitation or mental fumbling in his call to his countrymen to exert "force, force to the utmost, force without stint or limit" until peace was in fact achieved. He showed a good grasp of naval and military problems, and made a personal and valuable contribution to at least two major items of policy—the unification of military command, and the laying of an anti-submarine mine barrage in the North Sea.

But although the evident intention of Revolutionary Russia to retire from the war, culminating in the Treaty of Brest-Litovsk, increased the need for America's active participation, it was not until July 1917 that American troops landed in France, and they were not actually in the firing line until October. This time lag was partly a consequence of the inadequacy of the Preparedness policy, and partly due to the determination of Major-General John J. Pershing, now the American Commander-in-Chief, that American troops should fight as a separate Army under their own flag, and not, as the Allies urged, be mixed in with Allied units in small groups as and when they became equipped and available. During the critical months following the German offensive in March 1918, this demand was temporarily waived, but inevitably the deployment of the American Army was delayed until it could operate in force. It was not, in fact, until January 1918 that it took over a section of the Western Front.

In this, as in all other matters, Wilson stoutly supported Pershing. On balance he was almost certainly justified in his belief that this arrangement was the best way of maintaining at a high level American interest in the war. For we must remember that the original outbreak of the war had been unexpected, and to Americans inexplicable, that for nearly three years American participation in the war had been deplored, and that her actual entry into the war had not been accompanied by any dramatic event, such as the Pearl Harbour disaster, to rouse popular enthusiasm immediately to white heat. The slogan "All aid short of war" of the years before 1941 left fewer psychological barriers to be broken down than "All protests short of war" which might have been the motto for the years 1914 to 1917. Nevertheless, when these barriers were broken down, American troops took their full share of the fighting.

At home the declaration of war did not produce a suspension of party differences. In Congress a minority whose main strength lay in the Republicans of the East, but even included some Democrats, found it hard to believe that a Democrat was a proper person to be President, even in times of peace. In war such a situation appeared positively unnatural to a party which was disposed to regard victory in the Civil and Spanish-American Wars as a proof of its unique capacity to conduct wars to a successful issue. Particularly vehement was Theodore Roosevelt, who had been bitterly chagrined because Wilson supported the American War Department in their refusal to authorise him again to raise and lead a party of Volunteers. The Administration was accused of inefficiency and of not prosecuting the war with sufficient energy—of waging a phoney war, in fact. Republican Senators proposed that a War Cabinet should be established on a Coalition basis. Such a move would have prevented the Democrats from claiming sole credit for the successful conduct of a war greater than any conducted by Republicans, supposing that it should be successful.

But Coalitions are repugnant to the American political tradition, and Wilson, who was supported by the West and North-West, had little difficulty in winning a political victory in Congress by demanding and obtaining for himself the powers suggested for a Coalition War Cabinet. Laws were also passed authorising a censorship, not only of the press, but also of speech, establishing severe penalties for espionage (later used generally against "Reds" and Socialists), while Administrative Departments were set up, including a Food Administration under Herbert Hoover, and a War Industries Board under Bernard M. Baruch, who had under him Hugh S. Johnson and George Peek, later to play prominent parts in Franklin Roosevelt's New Deal. Muddles in the War Departments were cleared up by Edward R. Stettinius, father of the first American representative on the Council of U.N.O., who had handled Britain's munitions business with the House of Morgan, of which he was a partner. These appointments showed Wilson's evident willingness to place Republicans in important posts, but, nevertheless, the party was still resentful of its failure to obtain a formal partnership in the direction of the war, and was thus con-

firmed in its determination at all costs to win
the next Congressional elections as a first step
on the road back to power.

With America's entry into the war, although
as an Associated Power only, and not under any
Treaty of Alliance, all difficulties about
blockade or contraband incontinently dis-
appeared. The State Department made no bones
about forgetting its arguments in defence of
neutral rights, and fully justified the Secretary's
statement to the British Ambassador, "In three
months we shall be as great criminals as you
were!" The rigour of the blockade maintained
over Western Europe was, in fact, increased.

In the Far East, however, matters were not
so smooth. Japan had not been slow to perceive
that the war might be used to assist her ambitions in China. For the Allies the Japanese
alliance had the advantage that it released
British ships from the Pacific, while for the
Japanese it had the advantage that they were
able to secure German possessions in China, and
notably Shantung. In 1915 Japan presented to
China the notorious Twenty-one Demands
which gave her extensive powers over China and
constituted a gross violation of the Open Door.
Bryan had protested, but as he also recognised
that Japan had "special interests" in neighbour-
ing territories, his protest, not unnaturally, was
ineffective. By 1917, however, the advantages
of alliance with the Western Powers seemed to

Japan to be exhausted. She began to clamour for wider acquisitions in China, Borneo and the Dutch East Indies, and to toy with the idea of joining Germany, a move which might well have brought about a German victory. The tone of Wilson's Notes to Germany, so Tumulty asserts, prevented Japan actually leaving the Allies, and the American declaration of war at last gave them a trustworthy Pacific partner. But more seemed to be required than the material counterpoise of America's armed strength, and in 1917 Viscount Ishii came to the United States on a special mission, whose aim was to obtain a recognition of Japan's interests in China and a modification of the Open Door policy.

The result of this mission was the Lansing-Ishii Agreement of November 2nd, 1917, which reaffirmed the "Open Door," pledged both nations to respect China's political and territorial integrity and disclaimed any desire for special privileges. At the same time it recognised that

> "territorial propinquity creates special relations, and that Japan has special interests in China, particularly in that part to which her possessions are contiguous."

The Japanese were well content, for this recognition of their interests was substantial, while the affirmations and pledges were merely pious verbiage. It undoubtedly represented a real diplomatic victory and the beginning of the American retreat from the Far East which continued, despite Wilson, at Versailles, and quickened thereafter. In 1917, however, such concessions seemed a small price to pay for averting a German-Japanese alliance.

Wilson had from the first drawn a distinction between the German government and the German people. From his War Address to Congress onwards he reiterated that it was only for the German government that the United States had any hostility, while with the German people it had no quarrel. His speeches now had two objects—one to weaken the will to fight in the Central Powers, the other to establish a moral basis for peace on which both sides, the Allies included, would agree. Since he regarded the war as a struggle of the same nature as that which he had been waging at home, his speeches continued much the same line of thought as he had followed before America's entry into the war. They undoubtedly sapped the morale of the Central Powers, but they also caused no little heart-searching among the Allies.

The suggested bases of peace outlined in his speech of January 22nd, 1917, were further elaborated in a speech to Congress of January 8th, 1918, setting out Fourteen Points, constituting "the programme of the world's peace." They fall into three groups. The first five dealt in general terms with diplomacy, the freedom of the seas, economic conditions, disarmament and colonies. These were matters of general application, in which the various Powers had different degrees of interest. The next eight points dealt with particular territorial arrangements in Europe and the Ottoman Empire, some of which (particularly those suggested for the Balkans) were informed rather by optimism than by knowledge. Also, in view of the subsequent horror inspired by the word "Bolshevism," the sincere welcome proposed for Russia "under institutions of her own choosing" makes strange reading. Finally, the fourteenth point enshrined a proposal for a general association of nations with mutual guarantees of political independence and territorial integrity. There is a clear relation between these proposals and the speeches of Wilson and Lodge two years earlier before the League to Enforce Peace.

The speech of January 8th was made against a background of the Russo-German negotiations at Brest-Litovsk and the failure of an inter-Allied conference at Paris to agree on peace terms. On Feburary 11th, after receiving the German and Austrian replies to his speech, Wilson again addressed Congress, traversing much the same ground as before and setting out "Four Principles" to be applied to any final settlement. On Independence Day (July 4th) at Washington's tomb at Mount Vernon, he addressed assembled diplomats and set out the "Four Ends" for which the associated peoples of the world were fighting, summed up in a single sentence—"The reign of law based upon the consent of the governed, and sustained by the organised opinion of mankind." Finally, on September 27th, 1918, in a speech in New York he set out "Five Particulars" necessary to convert into a practical programme the general thesis of a League of Nations formed to uphold a peace based on "justice that plays no favourites." If he condemned the Imperialism and ignored the territorial ambitions of the Allies, yet his concluding sentence was equally not without significance—"Germany is constantly intimating the 'terms' she will accept; and always finds that the world does not want 'terms.' It wishes the final triumph of justice and fair dealing."

These four speeches made up what has been called Wilson's Moral Offensive. In later days they would have been termed "Political Warfare," but whatever we may call them, their effect in undermining the resistance of the Central Powers cannot be doubted. The latter appreciated Wilson's implacable determination to achieve both victory in war and absolute impartiality in peace; and if capitulation was unavoidable, there was more hope for the peoples of Germany and Austria in an approach to Wilson than to the leaders of any of the other belligerents, whose views on a proper peace settlement would be frankly penal. So on October 6th Prince Max of Baden, the newly appointed Chancellor of Germany, requested Wilson to bring about a general armistice based on his Fourteen Points speech and on subsequent pronouncements. Wilson seems to have been taken by surprise, but, suspecting some trick, he resisted the obvious temptation to concede the German request immediately. He did not, however, resist the more subtle temptation to handle the matter himself, and he proceeded to probe the German position on his own without consulting his associates.

It must be conceded, however, that he conducted the subsequent exchange of Notes with consummate and even cold-blooded skill. His messages to Germany were intended to establish three points—that his principles were accepted as a basis of peace and that future discussions would only be on the details of their application; that these discussions would be with representatives of the German people and not with those who had hitherto dictated German policy; that Germany would evacuate all invaded territories and observe all humane usages of war while doing so. The terms of an armistice, he argued, were technical matters for the Allied military advisers, and should "fully protect the interests of the peoples involved and ensure to the associated governments the unrestricted ability to safeguard and enforce the details of peace to which the German government has agreed." It is not surprising that the German Army commanders regarded this as tantamount to a demand for unconditional surrender—and, in fact, Wilson emphatically stated that it would be a question of surrender, and not of negotiation, unless the German people threw out their old rulers, including the King of Prussia.

It was not until he had received assurances on these points that Wilson communicated the correspondence to the Allies. Whether they would accept him as their spokesman then depended on whether they would accept the Fourteen Points. Colonel House hurried to Europe, and tense discussion took place in Paris, for while many of the Points were acceptable, Great Britain could not accept the second, dealing with Freedom of the Seas, even though House, with Wilson's approval, threatened that if the Points were rejected the United States might make a separate peace. He was, however, finally convinced, and Wilson informed the German government that the Allies had agreed to his principles, subject to two reservations—viz. that the freedom of the seas should be discussed at the subsequent Peace Conference, and that the restoration by Germany of invaded territories should be interpreted as implying that compensation would be made by Germany for the damage done by land, by sea and from the air

to the civilian population of the Allies and their
property. In transmitting this agreement to the
Germans, Wilson accepted the interpretation
and referred the Germans to Foch for armistice
terms. This Note was signed on November 5th,
and on the same day were held the American
Congressional elections.

From the Republican point of view the
failure of their attack in 1917 made victory in
the 1918 elections essential if they were to
return to power in the Presidential contest two
years later. The Democrats had won every election since 1910, and under Wilson's Presidency
had had their first chance since the Presidency
of Andrew Jackson of showing their capacity for
leadership on a large scale. The fact that they
had been far from unsuccessful increased the
danger that they might establish themselves in
power, if not under Wilson, then under some
other President. That the importance of the
election was also recognised by the Democrats
was shown by the fact that on October 24th
Wilson himself issued an appeal "To My Fellow
Countrymen" to return a Democratic majority
to Congress, on the ground that a Democratic
defeat at this stage would appear to indicate a
division of loyalties within the United States
which would encourage the Central Powers and
proportionately depress the Allies. Although
such action was not unprecedented, he was
bitterly attacked by the Republicans on the

somewhat specious ground that the President should not engage in party politics. The appeal was, however, fruitless, and the Republicans improved their position in both Houses of Congress. In the House of Representatives their majority was increased. In the Senate they also obtained a majority, but of only two votes, so that the balance of power lay with semi-independent members, such as La Follette, who was largely dependent on the votes of the German population of Wisconsin.

The results of the election placed the Republicans in a strong position, to lay the foundations of the 1920 campaign by unremitting hostility to the President's policy for the next two years. It also was evidence of a sectional change of leadership from the agricultural South to the industrial North. This change was particularly and vitally evident in the composition of the Senatorial Committees, of which the Foreign Relations Committee would play a vital part in the consideration of any Peace Treaty. In this particular Committee Republican control was ensured by the corrupt return of Mr. Truman Newberry as Senator for Michigan, who although indicted by a Federal Grand Jury in March 1919, and the subject of a Senatorial investigation, nevertheless retained his seat for sufficient time to secure the Republican majority.

Wilson, however, still retained his confidence.

On November 11th he issued an announcement in the following terms:

> "Everything for which America fought has been accomplished. It will now be our fortunate duty to assist by example, by sober, friendly counsel and by material aid in the establishment of a just democracy throughout the world."

His own contribution of friendly counsel he proposed to make in person, and it was to the rather unsympathetic Senate that he announced on December 2nd his intention to participate personally in the Peace Conference in Paris. The reason he gave was that the Allied Governments desired his presence for the personal interpretation and application of the principles of peace laid down in his earlier speeches.

But it may well be doubted whether in this Wilson correctly interpreted the feelings of the Allied Governments, nor did he with complete accuracy express his own. In private conversation with members of his Cabinet he had explained that his decision to go to Paris was due to the fact that while he was fully conversant with the viewpoint of the American people, he knew less about the forces moving on the Continent of Europe, and had not sufficient confidence in the reports he might receive on these subjects if he remained in Washington. It was,

he felt, essential for him to be on the spot to
assess the desires of the European peoples,
carrying with him, as he would, an exact knowledge of the ideals and aspirations of the people
of the United States. It is certainly the case that
up to date Wilson had interpreted extraordinarily well the desires of his own countrymen. As Franklin K. Lane had said, "He is conscious of public sentiment—surprisingly so—
for a man who sees comparatively few people."
But he was now entering on a period during
which his comprehension of the desires of the
people of the United States would drift farther
and farther away from their somewhat drab
reality.

A further reason for his desire to go to Paris,
and one to which he gave expression in a remarkable address to the members of the mission
which accompanied him, was the belief that he
alone of all the delegates (and therefore the
United States alone of all countries) truly represented the hopes and aspirations of the peoples
of the world. The American delegation, he
advised them, would therefore have to fight the
other delegates, whose motives were so much
lower than their own, while he himself would
act as the spokesman of humanity. It is said
that during this period of his life Wilson
developed a strong interest in Indian philosophy. The increasingly idealistic character
of his speeches and his growing belief in a

mysterious force emanating from humanity,
which crystallised into public opinion, may be
evidence of this. He clearly regarded as insigni-
ficant the vehement pronouncement by Theodore Roosevelt on November 27th to the effect
that the Republican victory in the elections
implied a repudiation by the American people
of Wilson's leadership, and deprived him of
authority to speak for the United States in any
representative capacity. But at any rate the
world had been warned.

Wilson and the other representatives—
Colonel House, Lansing, General Bliss and
Henry White (the last a Republican diplomat
from the McKinley–Theodore Roosevelt period)
—sailed on December 4th, 1918. Before the
opening of the Conference Wilson made a short
tour through Great Britain, France and Italy,
being hailed in all quarters as a political
Messiah, ushering in, at any rate, a new earth,
if not a new heaven. From Wilson's point of
view the tour enabled him both to generate
public opinion in favour of the principles which
he desired to see adopted in the ultimate Peace
Treaty, and himself to accumulate strength
from the expression of such opinion. In international conferences, however, the support of
public opinion is not always enough, and it
may even be ambiguously expressed. While the
peoples of their various countries were cheering
Wilson, at the same time in England Lloyd

George had won a resounding electoral victory on a platform by no means favourable to Wilsonian idealism, and Clemenceau in France had received an equally resounding vote of confidence from the French Chamber. Inasmuch as both of these leaders had by comparison with Wilson an insecure tenure of office, these votes of confidence were proportionately the more important in strengthening their position at the Conference, while Wilson, although for the time being personally irremovable, could not be regarded, except by those prepared to ignore the niceties of the American Constitution, as being in a wholly unequivocal position.

The details of the negotiations in Paris have been widely discussed and will not be pursued here. Our main interest will be directed to that part of the Treaty which was of most importance to Wilson—viz. the Covenant of the League of Nations. The hope of such a League had been vaguely put forward by President Grant, and expressed with some particularity at the meeting of the League to Enforce Peace held in May 1916, to which we have already referred. It had also been advocated by Theodore Roosevelt in his acceptance of the Nobel Peace Prize in May 1910. It was, in fact, an idea which had been worked upon for some time on both sides of the Atlantic, and by persons of all parties, by Colonel House and his staff and also by ex-President Taft, and on the British side by Lord

Phillimore, Sir Robert Cecil and others. In the course of discussions at Paris between representatives of the British and American delegations, these various plans had been combined in a general document, and the result was submitted to a Drafting Commission of the Conference, of which Wilson was Chairman. The plan provided for general disarmament, for international cooperation in the League Council and the League Assembly, and for the guidance and control of undeveloped peoples, and Wilson, ably assisted by General Smuts and Sir Robert Cecil, had the satisfaction of piloting the plan through the Commission substantially in the form which he himself desired. He was insistent that it should form an integral part of the Treaty of Peace, and this insistence, although a prime cause of America's failure to ratify the Treaty, was probably right on two grounds. First, in view of the speed with which the Treaty was being worked out and the inevitably hurried decisions which were being taken on the territorial demands of the various Allies, some device for making subsequent adjustments in the terms of the Treaty was obviously essential. Second, however, and more important from Wilson's point of view, it was essential to provide some bond which would almost automatically compel sovereign States to join the League of Nations, and the obvious way of doing this was to incorporate the Covenant in the Treaty which they would subsequently sign. It is worth remembering that at that date there was no such extraordinary compulsion as the invention of the atomic bomb to dramatise before the nations of the world the vital necessity for international co-operation.

The success of these early discussions made it easier for Wilson to return home in February 1919, as indeed he needed to do in order to attend to domestic business. The Assistant Secretary of the Navy, Franklin D. Roosevelt, is said to have intervened at a critical moment to navigate the *George Washington* safely through the dense fog which enveloped its destination, an episode which may be regarded as prophetic.

On arrival, Wilson gave some account of the progress made and stressed particularly and somewhat rashly his determination that the League should be an integral part of the Peace Treaty. As it stood, the Covenant made no mention either of the Monroe Doctrine nor of the Japanese demand for racial equality, which had been one of the questions most vigorously debated in the Drafting Commission. To the American Senate the unqualified participation of the United States in international affairs was highly displeasing, and in addition to a general attack on the League by Senator Knox, there was the particular demand that nothing in the Covenant should interfere with the operations of the Monroe Doctrine, or with the right of the

United States to withdraw from the League at any moment. Republican opinion, however, was not unanimous in opposition to the League, which was supported by ex-President Taft, who, however, warned Wilson that stronger opposition was to be expected later, and urged his acquiescence in the amendments proposed by the Senate. That this opposition would be strong was indicated by a Senate filibuster on an important Appropriation Bill, a Senatorial technique which was almost becoming a routine.

On March 4th Wilson returned to Paris, where he found the Allied Powers proposing to separate the Treaty from the Covenant. To such a proposal he was, of course, violently opposed, but the fact that he himself was now demanding certain concessions as required by the United States Senate meant that he too must yield on certain issues if he was to carry his main point. From Clemenceau came the demand for an alliance of the United States, Britain and France against Germany, the withholding of recognition from the new Russian government until debts to France were paid, the separation of Austria and Germany, indemnities and the Rhine frontier. From Italy came the demand for Fiume, and from the Japanese the demand for racial equality and the retention of Shantung. The United States clearly could not compel Russia to pay its debts, and the separation of Austria and Germany violated the principles of self-determination. Yet if the Covenant were to be amended in the sense demanded by American opinion, Wilson must yield something to the views of the other Allies.

In the middle of these complex and embittered discussions Wilson, on April 3rd, fell ill, a premonition of the stroke which he suffered in the following September. It is rather significant that after this episode Wilson became increasingly unyielding and obstinate in his judgments, not only of the international situation, but also of the political situation at home. In order to force a breach of the deadlock which was clearly developing, he summoned the *George Washington* to take him home. At this Clemenceau yielded his demand for the Rhine frontier, and Wilson in return agreed to Clemenceau's demand for an alliance. Japan was somewhat grudgingly awarded Shantung, but Wilson maintained his opposition to the Italian acquisition of Fiume, and went so far as to issue an appeal to the people of Italy over the heads of the Italian government. The fact that the Allies could not afford the Conference to fail forced them to accept the modifications in the original Covenant which Wilson required as a sop to Congressional opinion, although the logical French mind recoiled from a "Covenant" with its implied binding obligations, from which, nevertheless, it was possible to retire at will. On April 28th the Plenary Session of the

Conference accepted the Treaty incorporating the Covenant of the League of Nations, and it was finally signed on June 28th.

On June 29th Wilson sailed for America, arriving in New York on July 8th. Two days later he presented the Treaty to the Senate, by whom it would have to be ratified by a two-thirds majority in order to become effective and binding upon the United States. Since the Democrats numbered forty-seven, as against forty-nine Republicans, there was no chance of Wilson immediately obtaining such a majority, for even some members of his own party—e.g. Gore of Oklahoma, and Walsh of Massachusetts —were opposed to the Treaty and Covenant as it then stood.

The Republicans were divided into three groups. There was firstly the so-called "Battalion of Death," a body of some fourteen Senators irreconcilably opposed to a League of Nations in any shape or form. They included Philander C. Knox, of Pennsylvania, who had been Taft's Secretary of State, Medill McCormick of Illinois, a violent isolationist, Albert B. Fall of New Mexico, later to be involved in the "Teapot Dome" oil scandal, and survivors of the Progressive party, such as Hiram W. Johnson of California and William E. Borah of Idaho, who did not share Wilson's belief that the war had simply been a transference to a wider field of that fight against reaction at home which they had carried on together. As a group they combined ability, eloquence (Borah could be counted on to fill not only the floor of the Senate, but, more important, the galleries) and lack of scruple, and they were determined to defeat the Covenant by any and every means. They were prepared, therefore, to threaten to bolt the party either in 1919 or, worse still, in the Presidential election of 1920, should this appear necessary.

Next was a body of some twenty Senators, led by Henry Cabot Lodge, and including sound party hacks, like Warren Gamaliel Harding of Ohio, who would only accept the Covenant subject to strong reservations—that is to say, outright amendments of a kind that would need to be formally accepted by the other signatory Powers.

Finally, there was a batch of moderate reservationists, some twelve in number, including Senator Kellogg (later Secretary of State), who would be prepared to accept the League subject to certain mild reservations which would interpret or protect United States interests, but were hardly of a character to require the amended document to be resubmitted to the other signatories.

Although ratification required a two-thirds majority, the preliminary adoption of reservations required a simple majority only. If, therefore, the Democrats were to ally with the moderate reservationists, the outright amendments which the Lodge group desired could be defeated, and the mild reservations carried, despite the position of the irreconcilables. The remainder of the Republican party would then be left with the choice of either joining the mild reservation section or defeating outright a Treaty in which United States interests appeared to have been adequately safeguarded. Unfortunately, however, Wilson ultimately rejected the idea of reservations, or of any alliance with the moderates, who therefore followed their party loyalties and at the critical moment supported Lodge and rejection.

A further factor influencing the conduct of the Senate in respect of the Treaty was the shadow of the 1920 Presidential election. Even during the period of war politics in America had been returning to their normal pattern, and the conclusion of the military armistice had ended such political armistice as might have existed during the period of military hostilities. The Republicans were thus prepared to play politics in their most extreme and pure form in order that Wilson's leadership might be destroyed.

Some other elements in opposition to the Treaty may also be noted. In Paris Wilson had failed to secure self-determination for Ireland, although he had been instrumental at some embarrassment to himself in securing from the British a passage for an American delegation to visit Dublin, where its peculiar behaviour is stated to have been due to over-indulgence in Irish whisky. For this failure, and because in carrying through the Covenant Wilson had worked hand in hand with the British, the resulting document was opposed by the Irish-Americans, always more Hibernian than the inhabitants of Ireland itself. Other racial groups also opposed the Treaty—for example, the German-Americans for fairly obvious reasons, and the Italian-Americans, led by Fiorello La Guardia (later to become Director-General of U.N.R.R.A.), in resentment at Wilson's efforts to keep Italy out of Fiume.

The Treaty was also generally opposed by the American Liberals. Being unaware of, or preferring to ignore, the practical problems which Wilson had to meet in Paris, they demanded a perfect settlement of the world's evils, and regarded Wilson as having sold out his ideals and as having been duped by unscrupulous foreign diplomats. The *New Republic* published *"The Economic Consequences of the Peace,"* by John Maynard Keynes, which was extremely effective in mobilising opinion to the view that the Treaty was too severe.

Despite these various forces, however, American public opinion in general was not unfavourable to the Treaty. Opposition centred on Article X of the Covenant, and on the fear that the United States would need to take some responsibility for world affairs, and thus become involved in further wars. But even here Republican opinion was divided, for Taft supported Article X as merely extending the Monroe Doctrine to the world at large, and denied that it implied any necessary involvement of the United States in war. Wilson, of course, looked forward to increased American responsibility in world affairs: "We are provincials no longer." Apart from this issue the Republican opposition was primarily concerned to lay the foundations for a victory in the 1920 elections, and its technique was to prolong discussion in order to give themselves time to swing public opinion farther away from approval of the Treaty in the form in which a Democratic President had signed it. Although, therefore, Wilson had presented the text early in July, very little progress had been made by the end of August, although he had held several conferences with the Senate Foreign Relations Committee. As a result of this delay of two months Wilson's patience ran out, and he decided to undertake a tour, chiefly through the West, in order to rally and inform public opinion; as always, he assumed that public opinion would, when informed, rally to him.

It has been questioned whether this was a wise tactical move on Wilson's part. On the one hand, it may be urged that the real struggle was taking place in Washington, and that Wilson could have been far better employed in trying to bring his own direct and personal influence to bear upon individual Senators. He might well arouse enthusiasm in the West, but the final voting would take place on Capitol Hill. He had himself pointed out (in *Constitutional Government*) that an appeal to the people is likely to have less effect on the Senate than on the House of Representatives, but more than once before he had used this technique with success, and it is not difficult to see why he turned to it again. He set off on his tour on September 3rd, 1919, and in twenty-two days delivered forty addresses, which rank among the best of his speeches, although the preparation given to them was of the slightest. On September 26th at Wichita, Kansas, he collapsed with a stroke and returned to Washington. The tour, although a magnificent intellectual feat, was on the whole a failure. Only towards its close did Wilson succeed in arousing any substantial popular enthusiasm, and the tour perforce came to an end before this local enthusiasm had reached such a pitch as to be contagious. Moreover, it carried somewhat farther the breakdown of co-operation between President and Senate which had begun two years earlier.

Wilson's collapse gave rise to a peculiar constitutional problem which has, in fact, not yet been resolved. The Constitution provided that on the inability of the President to discharge his office, the Vice-President should take his place, but it did not lay down how this inability should be established. In these circumstances, despite the attempts made by the Republican opposition to displace Wilson, it was possible for him, with the assistance of Mrs. Wilson and his official family (his secretary, Tumulty, and Admiral Grayson, his doctor) to retain the reins of power in his hands, although for some time it was doubtful how far he was himself directing the governmental equipage.

It is also noticeable that throughout 1919 the more unpleasant characteristics of a moral reformer, from which he derives his strength—for example egotism—appear in Wilson to become more marked, and particularly after his return to Paris in March. By September he was no longer in communication with Colonel House, for reasons which are still obscure, but are apparently connected with the situation which he had found in Paris on his return. In February 1920 he dismissed Lansing, ostensibly on the ground that the Secretary of State had called Cabinet meetings in Wilson's absence. Lansing had, in fact, called meetings of Ministers, but these were informal discussions merely. They were obviously necessary for the conduct of business which Wilson was incompetent to transact, and were certainly very venial delinquencies. The real reason for Wilson's action was the revelation of some unfavourable but justified criticisms of the Treaty which Lansing had expressed in Paris. Wilson regarded this as personal treachery to himself, but he should have known the views of his Secretary of State before taking him to Paris. Once there, as the Treaty developed, Lansing's position became increasingly difficult, for to resign during the negotiations would have completely destroyed the position of the American delegation and any personal power on Wilson's part to achieve his aims. In the conduct of the campaign at home to secure the Senatorial endorsement of the Treaty, Wilson declined to relinquish control and became increasingly opposed to any compromise with the opposition although before he left on his speaking tour he had drafted four interpretative reservations which might have formed the basis for an alliance with the "mild reservationists."

At this time the political skill and suavity in negotiation of Colonel House would have been invaluable and Wilson's severance from his old friend and adviser was a major disaster. Yet House, though ill himself, did his best to play his accustomed rôle, and late in October sent to Washington Colonel Stephen Bonsal, who obtained from Lodge a statement of the minimum reservations that the latter would accept, which were of a relatively minor character. This document was promptly sent to Wilson, who neither acknowledged it nor acted on it. It is, in fact, uncertain whether he received it or whether it was kept from him by his official family.

Lodge was pardonably offended and five days later put forward fourteen reservations—their number apparently designed as a reflection on Wilson's Fourteen Points. In the main they were designed to exempt the United States from any obligation to support the actions of the League of Nations, to give her the privilege of unrestricted armament and to repudiate the Shantung award. A final reservation, designed to appeal to the Irish vote, urged that Ireland should speedily achieve a government of her own choice and be promptly admitted to membership of the League. These reservations were accepted by the Senate, but even so the Treaty failed to obtain the necessary number of votes.

During the ensuing winter public demand for ratification of the Treaty actually increased, and even Lodge began to weaken in his opposition to it until finally overborne by the Battalion of Death. Republicans such as Hoover and Taft, together with W. J. Bryan, urged ratification subject to mild reservations. But Wilson remained immovable and instructed the Democratic Senators to refuse any reservations and, if reservations were carried, to vote against the Treaty. He seems to have decided to adopt the strategy of creating a deadlock in the Senate in the hope that the mild reservationists would then join the Democrats to carry the Treaty in its original form, or else that public reaction against the Senate would enable the Democrats to carry the 1920 election, and so ratify the Treaty in the following year.

It is not mere wisdom after the event to suggest that this strategy was misconceived. In the first place, even were the Democrats to defeat all the Republican Senators who would be standing for re-election in 1920, it would still be mathematically impossible for them by themselves to command the necessary two-thirds majority. On the other hand, there was no particular reason to suppose that the mild reservationists would join the Democrats unless their mild reservations were accepted. But Wilson's final refusal of a possible alliance was brusque and merely served to confirm the mild reservationists in their party loyalty and cause them to vote with Lodge.

It is clear that Wilson's better strategy would have been to accept some at least, if not indeed all, of the reservations put forward by Lodge in October, and to leave the Republicans in the subsequent electoral campaign to deal with internal problems which in themselves were sufficiently difficult for any political party. The cost of living was rising, and this was affecting the cotton farmers and Western grain growers, two important elements in the strength of Wilson and the Democrats, while the industrial areas

were being swept by a wave of strikes and the
attempts of the I.W.W. to organise one big
union of all workers. Failing this, an alliance
with the "mild reservationists" would have
carried the Treaty with reservations which went
little, if at all, beyond the five favoured by
Hitchcock, the Democratic leader in the Senate,
four of which were Wilson's own. Wilson, however, evidently thought that reservations of any
kind would be dishonourable, and would probably merely be the prelude to further demands.
Moreover he seems to have overestimated the
influence of Republican leaders, such as Taft
and Hughes, and the extent to which public
opinion would in the last resort support the
Treaty.

Thus when, in March 1920, the Treaty was
again introduced into the Senate, the Republican party was able to carry the strong reservations which it desired, while on the final poll,
on March 19th, the negative votes of the Democrats, together with the Republican irreconcilables, were sufficient to ensure that the Treaty
should not secure the necessary majority, the
final voting being forty-nine for the Treaty to
thirty-five against. Among the latter were the
Republican Senators Hiram Johnson (California) and Capper (Kansas) and the Democrats
Gerry (Rhode Island), Walsh (Massachusetts)
and McKellar (Tennessee). On July 29th, 1945,
the four latter voted to ratify the United Nations

Charter, but Senator Johnson maintained his opposition, though he was too ill to vote.

Since this left the United States still technically at war with the Central Powers, the Senate in May abrogated the Declaration of War in a Resolution which Wilson promptly vetoed as a national disgrace. The Senate's action on the Treaty was pure politics in the American sense, designed to ensure the defeat of Wilson and the Democrats in the autumn Presidential election. For his part, Wilson now aimed at making the election a "grave and solemn referendum" upon the Treaty issue, but, in fact, it became, as forecast by the newspapers, a grave and solemn muddle.

The Treaty was not the only issue at that election. Among domestic problems were those of taxation, railroads and the price of wheat, while among foreign issues the acceptance or refusal by America of the Armenian mandate was also in question. Nor were the issues clearly set out, for the policies of the two parties on the Treaty and the Covenant were not clearly distinguishable. Voters were urged to support Governor Cox of Ohio and Franklin D. Roosevelt, the Democratic candidates for President and Vice-President, because they were followers of Wilson and upholders of the League of Nations, while they were also urged to vote for Harding, with Coolidge as Vice-President, because the Republicans would lead the country into a safe Association of Nations. Harding, in fact, succeeded in obtaining the support, not merely of Johnson of California, who was a rabid opponent of the Covenant, but also of Taft, who was a thoughtful and judicious supporter.

The election gave Harding the unprecedented plurality of 7 million votes, Governor Cox failing even to carry his own State, while of the Southern States, Tennessee voted for the Republican candidate. On the basis of Harding's speeches it was by no means clear that the American people had by their vote repudiated the Treaty and the League of Nations, but a party with a 7-million plurality feels entitled to put such interpretation as it pleases upon its election pledges, and after his inauguration no more was heard of the Covenant. In July 1921 Congress brought to an end the state of war with the Central Powers on terms which assured to the United States the advantages but none of the responsibilities of the Treaty of Versailles.

Woodrow Wilson and American Liberalism

WHEN Colonel Harvey in 1906 proposed Wilson for the Democratic Presidency, he did not foresee that fourteen years later he would be instrumental in nominating Wilson's Republican successor. Yet so it turned out, for not only the apparent ingratitude of his political protégé, but disappointment at the latter's policies, had caused the Colonel to seek the Republican fold, and on the night of June 11th, 1920, he was one of a small group of party leaders who met in the traditionally "smoke-filled" room 404 of the Hotel Blackstone in Chicago in an endeavour to break the deadlock in the Republican Convention. It was he who asked Senator Warren G. Harding whether there was any reason in his past life why he should not be nominated. Harding, doubtless reflecting that an illegitimate child had been no obstacle to the election of Cleveland, replied that there was not, and the leaders then forced his nomination through the Convention. "He was nominated," said Harvey, "because there

263

was nothing against him and because the delegates wanted to go home," but in the sequel it
was clear that his judgment of character had
not improved since the day he had picked Wilson as a harmless and complaisant figurehead
for the Democrats. However, he had his reward,
for in May 1921 Harding appointed him
Ambassador to Great Britain.

Wilson attended Harding's Inauguration—his
drawn and broken figure a sad contrast to his
athletic bearing eight years before and to the
sinister bonhomie of his so clearly mediocre
successor. After the ceremony he retired to a
small house in S Street, Washington. As if in
response to some curious inward hankering to
make a fresh start, he had formed another law
partnership—this time with his last Secretary of
State, Bainbridge Colby. But the breakdown in
his health was too extreme, and in any event
there were few cases which his sense of personal
integrity or the dignity of an ex-President would
allow him to accept. So the firm of Wilson and
Colby in its turn was dissolved and Wilson's
public career ended, as it had begun, with the
unsuccessful practice of the law. He died on
February 3rd, 1924.

In the twelve years that followed Harding's
election it might well be felt that Wilson's
Presidency had achieved nothing, that American
history had come full circle and that the country had returned to the position and frame of

mind in which it passed the years immediately following the Civil War. Both were periods of Republican dominance, of abundant industrial expansion coupled with falling farm income and ending in acute depression, with a prevailing conservatism in social philosophy. That no detail in the comparison might be lacking, the Presidency of Harding was characterised by administrative corruption and financial scandals which cast into the shade those of Grant's time and were accepted by the people with equal, if not greater, unconcern. It seemed as if all Wilson's efforts, indeed, those of Liberal reformers for the last generation, had gone for nothing, as Herbert Hoover, Secretary of Commerce and later President, reversed the policy embodied in the Sherman and Clayton Acts and encouraged the formation of trade associations to eliminate the waste and inefficiency, as he saw it, of free competition; as mergers and corporations grew apace and the House of Morgan again extended its financial control over approximately one-fourth of the corporate assets of the country. For this was the period when "the business of the United States is business," of "normalcy," and of "rugged individualism."

Wilson, no less than his three Republican successors, believed in individualism, but his view of the function of the State was very different. To him the duty of government was to promote free competition by eliminating

265

unfair practices and over-mighty interests, so that small businesses might become big and big businesses honest. In the Republican philosophy *laissez-faire* was more strictly interpreted, and while control was not objected to so long as business held the controls, government was expected to refrain from hampering business by regulations, and rather to nourish it with subsidies and tariffs. Thus in September 1922 the Fordney–McCumber tariff restored to the Payne–Aldrich level many duties that Wilson had reduced, and eight years later the Hawley–Smoot tariff raised them still farther. In foreign relations no party now advocated American membership of the League of Nations or co-operation between the United States and other countries. Indeed, even the Democratic party, which had campaigned in 1920 on the issue of the League, declined to endorse it in the party platform of 1924, despite an eloquent plea by Newton D. Baker. Among the delegations who voted against the League was the delegation from New York, of which Franklin D. Roosevelt was a prominent member. It is not without significance that the administration of Wilson's great Democratic successor was, at its inception, more nationalistic than that of the Republican Hoover.

In New Jersey the institution of the Direct Primary had, in the end, little effect upon the power of the party machines. After Wilson the

Conservative and business interests resumed their domination of the State, the municipal ownership of public utilities was defeated, the organisation of labour hampered and the modernisation of the archaic tax system delayed. By 1920 practically nothing was left of the "Seven Sisters" Bill. Princeton still has its Clubs and lacks its Quadrangles.

But before we rule out Wilson as a failure, there is much to be said on the other side. We must consider his personal success as a politician, his influence on the Democratic party and his relation to American Liberalism.

That Wilson was a very shrewd politician was a fact which escaped the professionals who first raised him to power. At his best he was both astute and daring and, at need, tough and uncompromising. To be sure, there were expedients to which he would not stoop—for example, in 1920 he refused to take advantage of the report that Harding had negro blood in his veins; it was baseless, anyway. But at Princeton he had not hesitated to point out that President Patton's retention of British citizenship hampered his comprehension of the character of American youth; he did not shrink from threatening a separate peace with Germany in order to force his Fourteen Points on the Allies, and he contemplated the use of America's financial strength after the war to compel Europe to America's way of thinking. At Princeton his success in raising the academic standard was undeniable, while the accuracy of his diagnosis of the problem presented by the Clubs was later recognised both there and in other universities, who also adopted, in one form or another, his solution. In New Jersey, where he first showed his mettle in public as distinct from university politics, the success with which he moulded the Legislature to his will and got on to the Statute Book the legislation that he had programmed was the more remarkable in view of the constitutionally weak position of the State Governor, who could not hold office for two consecutive terms. Wilson showed what could be done even in one term by a tough and inflexible reformer, and at the least he did succeed in breaking the New Jersey pre-eminence as the home of corporations.

The traditional limitation of the Presidency to two terms was a similar disadvantage to Wilson at the White House. Since rivalry between the Executive and the Legislature is the normal state of American politics, more than two consecutive terms are needed if a President is to establish his authority over Congress or secure any sort of continuity for his policy. Any President who has taken a strong line during his first term inevitably finds Congressional opposition intensified during his second, and particularly after the mid-term elections. Had his health remained good or the war broken out during his second term rather than his first, Wilson might have challenged the third-term tradition with success. What the consequences would have been for the world it would be interesting but futile to speculate. But it is worth recalling that he had already provided America with the sufficiently unusual spectacle of a President who not merely announced his policy, but actually carried it out, and had shown an hitherto unequalled control of Congress, brought about by a mixture of argument, mastery of legislative detail, well-designed appeals to the public and unabashed use of the Democratic machine—the "Old Guard" who "stand without hitching."

To have got the programme of his Inaugural Address embodied in legislation within nineteen months was an astounding achievement for a relative newcomer at the political game. While earlier reformers and Progressives had talked about reform, Wilson wrote it into the Federal Statute Book, where, despite some subsequent reversals, much yet remains. In foreign affairs the "grape-juice diplomacy" of himself and Bryan began that fundamental transformation of American foreign policy towards Latin-America which was to bear its full fruit only in the next generation, and if he may be criticised for having cast America for too idealistic a rôle in world affairs, we should at least pay tribute to the tenacity with which he expounded the view that she had in truth a rôle to play.

It has often been suggested that he was out-witted by the subtle diplomats of Europe during the discussions at Paris. But it is as often forgotten that it was during his second visit, when his position had been undermined by events at home, that he was forced to make the concessions for which he was later reproached, and even then he successfully resisted the more extreme demands of the victorious Powers. During his first visit, in discussions lasting less than a month, he got embodied in the draft Treaty the Covenant of the League of Nations substantially as he had envisaged it, and the fact that in this he was supported by such men as General Smuts and Lord Robert Cecil by no means detracts from his personal achievement. The most constructive and forward-looking element in the Treaty was indubitably Wilson's work.

Moreover, although the Republicans repudiated the idea of Wilson's League, they were prepared to co-operate in practice. As early as 1922 the United States began to send unofficial observers to League Conferences on social problems, and three years later the country was officially represented at the Conference on the traffic in arms and munitions. Thereafter the co-operation of the United States was continuous, and their willingness to support the efforts of the League to enforce peace was emphasised by successive Secretaries of State. To be sure, other nations might well wonder whether, in an emergency, they could count on a practical manifestation of that willingness. But the blame for this should not be laid at Wilson's door, but rather at that of the Senate, which, among other things, consistently refused American adherence to the World Court despite recommendation by successive Presidents and the anomalous fact that from the beginning one of the judges had been an American. In this light there is much significance in Wilson's later reflection, shortly before his death, that America's entry into the League, had it taken place in 1920, might have been merely a personal victory for himself and would not have proceeded from the conviction that it was the right thing for the country to do; only when the country was so convinced would it be the right time for it to join.

His influence on the Democratic party must not be overlooked. That a Democratic President had been able to hold Executive power for two consecutive terms was a remarkable fact in the party's history, and that during that time it had proved its capacity to govern efficiently both in peace and war was a revelation for which the country was not prepared, conditioned as it had been to years of Republican dominance. But these aspects were perhaps the least important. Far more significant was the fact that Wilson gave to a party that was highly impatient of control a firm leadership and, what is more, made the party like it. True, the old machine leaders increasingly resented the loss of local autonomy which was implied in Wilson's concept of responsible leadership, but the acclamation with which he was renominated in 1916 showed the extent to which the party as a whole welcomed the new regime. In a negative sense, the confusion of the 1920 election and the fact that in 1924 the party repeated the mistake of twenty years earlier in trying to beat the Republicans with a Conservative showed its necessity. Thus the way was paved for the next Democratic President and his successful breach of the third-term tradition.

No less important than this leadership was the extent to which Wilson advanced the conversion of the party from an advocacy of State Rights to an intelligent nationalism. Sectional the party might be, and dependent on the alliance of the South and West, whose renewal was another of Wilson's triumphs, yet Wilson saw and impressed upon the party an appreciation of the needs of the nation as a whole and of the duty of the government to serve the whole people, not merely one part of it. Himself singularly free from sectional influence, pride in his country was one of the mainsprings of his policy, national and international. Hence arises the paradox that the strongest measures of centralised government sprang from a party conceived in State Rights and dedicated to the proposition that Federal power must be restricted. That government is the servant of the people, and not of particular interests, was not one of the truths which Americans held to be self-evident. Wilson not only had preached this doctrine during the latter part of his academic career, but he brought his party to the practice of it and gave the country its first real taste of its application on a wide scale. It was Wilson's tragedy that he carried the doctrine of service to a point where the people were not prepared to follow him. To justify this judgment we must analyse Wilson's relationship to the course of American Liberalism.

Liberalism in America, though drawing inspiration from both Britain and France, was moulded into a form different from that prevailing in either country by the presence of the frontier atmosphere and the absence of an aristocracy, so that America was, for the first century of its independent existence, a genuinely classless country. Hence it embodies the emotional attachment to individualism and equality which is so strong as to amount to a fundamental American belief. Decisions on the frontier are essentially individual, and governmental functions are thus reduced to the maintenance of individual liberties. Even when the practical problems against which Liberalism constituted the reaction shifted from the frontier to the city, individualism remained the basic concept, though somewhat altered in its practical application by the change from a rural to an urban setting. The alteration has been variously described as from political to economic Liberalism or from American to entrepreneurial Liberalism. Political or American Liberalism stands firmly on equality, the denial of the right of any one individual to wield power over another, and from its rural background regards the liberty of the individual as a positive fact implying both effort and responsibility. Economic Liberalism, on the other hand, the doctrine of enlightened self-interest erected into a system of society, contributes little to the maintenance of either economic or social equality, indeed rather presumes that the market relations between individual competitors will be determined by their economic inequality.

In the United States, whether as a view of society or a system of belief, economic Liberalism became associated with the urban and industrial elements for whom the content of individual liberty is the negative one of freedom from controls and from responsibility for social conditions. In so far as these two forms of Liberalism may, in America, be identified respectively with rural and urban society, to that extent we may regard much of American history as determined by the contrast and frequent opposition between them, the former representing the American tradition which demands from the government positive action to maintain equality between individuals, the latter barring action to abate economic inequality or to ameliorate its consequent evils. Although there was always sufficient common belief in *laissez-faire* as a principle to cause the two to become confused in American thought, yet this contrast is not an undue simplification and provides a useful clue to the various political movements in which American Liberalism embodied itself.

For it must be made clear that Liberalism was never the underlying philosophy of any single American political party, but is rather a body of sentiment from which from time to time the major parties in turn draw contributions, reform on Liberal lines being no more confined to Democrats than to Republicans. The so-called Liberal Republican party is the exception that proves the rule, for it came together on a basis of practical proposals rather than of political philosophy. Both the Populist and Progressive movements grew out of the rural resistance to the over-mighty power of urban industrial enterprise and finance, and both sought to protect the American tradition of individualism and equality by political devices against the social and economic forces by which these were threatened. But it is significant that while during the period under review British Liberalism, faced with analogous problems, was aiming to moderate the effects of individualistic competition and was tending more and more to schemes of social control, American Liberalism aimed to preserve individualistic competition and maintained its belief in private enterprise.

Wilson's Liberalism was born in the English classical tradition. At home he could have read the *Edinburgh Review* and also *The Nation,* an American journal which, under E. L. Godkin, was Gladstonian in its outlook. At college he read widely among English political writers, of whom Burke and Bagehot were his favourites. His reading was, indeed, chiefly political; although at Johns Hopkins he did read a considerable amount of economics, he was not much interested in economic analysis, and it is doubtful whether in that sphere he ever really moved from his earliest position "pretty much of the old Manchester School—to the right of John Stuart Mill." In his earlier years on the Princeton Faculty he upheld the principles of pure economic Liberalism, the virtues of private initiative and the necessity of individualism, particularly the need to rely on the enlightenment of the individual to produce the desired social and economic conditions. But the disputes over the Clubs and Quadrangles caused him to change his views, and by 1910 he was in a fair way of abandoning in favour of positive political action the individualism that had commended him to the "sound bankers and Democrats who have been voting the Republican ticket." By the time he reached the White House he had rejected the theory that permits unrestricted individualism to proceed to the self-destructive conclusion of cut-throat competition. Wilson's solution to the trust problem was not through regulation by a Hamiltonian central government, as Theodore Roosevelt advocated, but a return to a Jeffersonian competitive society, where economic liberty and equality is guaranteed by regulating not monopoly, but competition, so that it may be genuinely free competition. His dilemma was very like that of John Stuart Mill—namely, how to maintain the economic liberty of the individual and the self-respect of the working man without compromising economic progress. The solution for both seemed to be adherence to the principles of private capitalism and free competition, while making such exceptions as might seem necessary to preserve fundamental human decencies.

Wilson too had his own contribution to make to American Liberalism, which gives the measure of his significance for the movement. First, he provided a coherent and articulated philosophy set out most compactly in the series of campaign speeches collected in *The New Freedom*. The essence of his views is expressed in the quotation from the Jackson Day Speech given in an earlier chapter—namely, to set the government of the country free and the business of the country free and to restore to the people of the country the freedom to control their own affairs. In this light the various concrete proposals which he wrote into the Federal Statute Book fall logically into place as part of a single scheme. But Liberalism is a "comprehensive" creed, in that it refuses to separate national and international problems. Gladstone, who was Wilson's ideal, had said that the first foundation for a good foreign policy is a good policy at home—and Wilson held the converse to be equally true. Second, therefore, Wilson aimed to guarantee in the international sphere the same degree of morality and economic freedom as he sought to establish at home. Whatever might be the immediate occasion of America's entry into the World War, for Wilson its ultimate aim was to save the world from domination by autocracy, militarism and plutocracy. From this point of view America's declaration of war is the climax of Wilson's Liberalism. And just as in domestic affairs Wilson advocated government action to ensure freedom for and between individuals—Adam Smith's "invisible hand" not being alone sufficient—so too, in the international sphere and for the same reasons, he advocated an international organisation to guarantee conditions of freedom for and between nations.

The realisation that corporate action was needed to secure individual freedom was the inevitable consequence of the fundamental defect of nineteenth-century Liberalism, which may be summed up by saying that it succeeded in creating units, but failed to create unity. Both in the national and international sphere the benefits that flowed from the emphasis on individual freedom were bought at the cost of the sacrifice of a sense of social unity, call it a family system, in which the individual, whether citizen or nation, found an assured place. To say that this system, nationally and internationally, was reactionary and that the destruction of domestic feudalism and the Holy Alliance were alike justified, is no real answer. For the loss of that sense of belonging to an association of which the whole is somehow greater than the sum of its parts was real, and neither Canning and Monroe in the international sphere nor Adam Smith and Ricardo in the domestic offered anything to replace it. Thus Wilson's appeal to his countrymen to realise what they owed to their country, his profound sense that the claims of America transcended those of sectionalism and that in the nation's service the individual could find perfect freedom, was an attempt to fill the gap that Liberalism had created. Similarly, in international affairs the Covenant of the League of Nations was to provide individual nations with a bond of common service to humanity. But to this call to a wider service his countrymen were not yet ready to respond.

Thus Wilson grasped the problem of the twentieth century, but his solution was of the nineteenth—to repair (or internationally, to provide) the machinery of democratic government, and then his country and all countries would thrive. His stress on the need for Executive leadership and close relations between President and Congress accurately diagnosed the weakness of the American form of government. But his remedy was only partial, for more radical reforms were necessary to achieve his aim of increasing the ability of the people to use the government to promote their own welfare. Social and economic changes had gone too far to be countered by mere political devices in a simple Jeffersonian democracy which is powerless in the face of great economic or financial concentrations. American democracy could only be preserved by a return to an even simpler economic society than the freely competitive capitalism at which Wilson aimed. Such a return was impracticable, but the alternative—a new social order and form of government suitable to a modern industrialised State—was beyond Wilson's horizon and that of his contemporaries, who wanted the best of both worlds—a Jeffersonian democracy and millionaires. So, too, in international relations equality of all nations is impossible when there are "Great Powers," and a simple return to the prescriptions of the Manchester School—the removal of obstacles to intercourse, free access to raw materials and freedom of the seas—will not be enough.

That Wilson saw the problem of his age—as it is of ours—but could not provide a permanent solution was due as much to his temperament as to his training. Besides his pride in America, to which reference has already been made, he was also driven onwards by his conscience and his idealism. These great qualities were accompanied by their characteristic defects. Although it is an exaggeration to say that he was unable to be conciliatory to an opponent or talk him round, he could be hard and uncompromising, and particularly when he thought that a principle was involved, because then more than ever he believed that he was right and that those who disagreed with him were positively immoral. A scholar, he would seek opinions, but in the end would rather delve into his own mind, and from consciousness of his own resources he drew the self-confidence that was the source of his power. Thus, while he was unequalled in rallying disinterested men to his side, he was not able to bind them by personal ties of loyalty, for he could not endure disagreement from those whom he believed to be his friends. He believed that the mass of the people was capable of sharing his high idealism of service, ignoring that in most cases they will judge a policy, as a Tammany politician put it, "by what's in it for Mrs. Murphy and the kids"; as has been said, he failed to take a sufficiently cynical view of humanity, a fault the present generation finds it difficult to condone.

But Smuts's judgment that "it was not Wilson who failed at Paris, it was humanity" is not fair to Wilson or to humanity. Humanity cannot be reproached for acting according to its nature, and Wilson did not fail at Paris. His failure came later, during those last months when his career appears as a truly Greek Tragedy, the tragedy of the honest man driven by an inward compulsion to a course of action which the audience alone can see to be fatal. During these months his consciousness of right, his idealism, his confidence that this idealism was shared by his countrymen, all blinded him to the sordid facts that the Treaty was not the unalloyed triumph that he claimed it to be, that even if it were, it was not therefore universally acceptable, that his control of Congress was not what it had been in the earlier years of his Presidency and that management and compromise were necessary.

As a result, his fall from the summit of international prestige was even more rapid than his ascent, fast though that had been. His opposition to national claims, such as those of the Italians to Fiume and of the French to the left bank of the Rhine, destroyed his popularity with those countries, while his reputation as a Liberal leader suffered from his failure firstly to attain the peace of conciliation which he had promised, and then to persuade his own country to accept the more limited settlement which, in fact, he secured. Had he presented the Treaty to the United States, not as something identical with the ideals he had set out to achieve, but as the best that could be obtained within the limits of the possible, he might have had better success; but he allowed his political acumen to be swamped by pursuit of the ideal. Nevertheless, it is undeniable that the sole creative act of the Peace Conference, which was the League of Nations, resulted from Wilson's leadership.

And yet, in the last analysis, was his faith in the "sober second thought" wholly unjustified, even though it may take the nations longer to reach it than he had hoped?

We may find a clue in the words of his friend and Princeton colleague, Bliss Perry:

> "He had worked tirelessly in solitude, had held himself inflexibly to his task. He had learned self-reliance. He trusted his own logic and his own instincts without much counsel from other men. It is the ancient story of heroes—and of martyrs."

Or in the words of Mrs. Eleanor Roosevelt after the death of President Franklin Roosevelt:

> "Woodrow Wilson was also stricken and, in that instance, the peoples of the world failed to carry out his vision.

"Perhaps in His wisdom, the Almighty is trying to show us that a leader may chart the way, may point out the road to lasting peace, but that many leaders and many peoples must do the building. It cannot be the work of one man, nor can the responsibility be laid upon his shoulders, and so, when the time comes for peoples to assume the burden more fully, he is given rest."

But let the last word be Wilson's own:

"Ideas live, men die."

Bibliography

Books marked with an asterisk contain further
bibliographies.

I. WOODROW WILSON

The Life and Letters of Woodrow Wilson, by
Ray Stannard Baker, 8 vols. (Doubleday, Doran &
Co. Inc., 1927–39), is the authorised life and
invaluable; to be supplemented by *The Public
Papers of Woodrow Wilson*, ed. R. S. Baker and
W. E. Dodd, 6 vols. (Harper & Bros., 1926).

For the development of Wilson's ideas: *The
Political Education of Woodrow Wilson*, by James
Kerney (The Century Co., 1926; *The Origins of
the Foreign Policy of Woodrow Wilson*, by Harley
Notter (Johns Hopkins Press, Baltimore, 1937);
The Economic Thought of Woodrow Wilson, by
William Diamond (Johns Hopkins Press, Balti-
more, 1943).

For the War of 1914: *Woodrow Wilson and the
World War*, by C. Seymour (Yale University Press,
1921); *The Life and Letters of Walter H. Page*, ed.
Burton J. Hendrick, 3 vols. (Heinemann, 1923–6);
The Intimate Papers of Colonel House, arranged
as a narrative by C. Seymour, 4 vols. (Benn,
1926–8).

Woodrow Wilson and the Lost Peace and
Woodrow Wilson and the Great Betrayal, by T. A.
Bailey (Macmillan & Co., 1944 and 1945), for the

Peace Conference and the ultimate failure of the
Senate to ratify the Treaty of Versailles.

Woodrow Wilson and the People, by H. C. F.
Bell (Doubleday, Doran & Co. Inc., 1945), is the
most recent and best study of Wilson.

II. AMERICAN HISTORY

The Epic of America, by J. T. Adams
(Routledge, 1938), for the drama of American
history. *The Growth of the American Republic,*
by S. E. Morison and H. S. Commager (O.U.P., 3rd
ed., 1942), 2 vols. (origins to December 9th, 1941).

For special aspects of American history:
Economic History of the American People, by E.
L. Bogart and D. L. Kemmerer (Longmans, Green
& Co., 1942); *A Diplomatic History of the United
States,* by S. F. Bemis (H. Holt & Co., 2nd ed.,
1942); *Short History of the American Labour
Movements,* by Mary Beard (Macmillan, 1920); *The
American Political System,* by D. W. Brogan
(Hamish Hamilton, 2nd ed., 1943).

The Autobiography of Lincoln Steffens (Harcourt
Brace, 1931) gives much of the atmosphere of the
period and *The American Procession,* by Agnes
Rogers and Frederick Lewis Allen (Harper & Bros.,
1933) the illustrations.

The Dictionary of American Biography (Scrib-
ners, 1943–4).

III. DOCUMENTS

Speeches and Documents in American History,
ed. Robert Birley (O.U.P. World's Classics), Vols. 3
and 4, and a wider selection in *Documents of
American History,* ed. H. S. Commager (F. S. Crofts
& Co., 3rd ed., 1943).

Index

287

INDEX